I MET MYSELF IN OCTOBER

A MEMOIR OF BELONGING

JACOB TAYLOR-MOSQUERA

For Cindy, my one and only real mother,
with enduring admiration and love.

“The most difficult thing in life is to know yourself.”

\- Thales

ISBN: 978-1-09831-409-5 (print)

ISBN: 978-1-09831-410-1 (ebook)

CONTENTS

FOREWORD

WHETHER YOU ARE AWARE OF IT OR NOT, CHANCES are you are a member of the adoption constellation. This consists of anyone who knows or is related to someone in the community who has experienced an adoption. Statistically, one in every six people in the United States are directly impacted by adoption. This means they themselves, a family member or a close friend has been adopted, has adopted a child, or has placed a child for adoption (Evan B. Donaldson Institute, 1997). With those odds, you are likely connected to adoption in some manner.

By now, you have thought of someone in your life: a friend, neighbor, coworker, significant other, coach, grandparent, etc. to whom you are connected to that fits the adoption triad (adoptee, first/birth parent, adoptive parent) demographic which, in turn, makes you a member of the adoption constellation! If this is new knowledge to you, then we welcome you. Similarly, if you have always identified as a member of the adoption constellation, then I do not need to convince you why "I Met Myself in October: A Memoir of Belonging" will speak to all of us who have ever experienced the struggle of belonging.

Hello, my name is Astrid Castro and I am the Founder and Director of Adoption Mosaic. At Adoption Mosaic, we spend extensive time building bridges with adoption communities for forward-thinking dialogue on adoption-related topics while offering support and education to those who are learning what it means to be a part of the adoption constellation.

Part of my life's work over more than thirty years has been dedicated to creating adoptee panels, a platform which offers space for individuals to share their adoption experiences with others. When I began this work in 1990 as a 19-year-old, I had to find and build my own community. I soon discovered that we adoptees had not been invited to share our experiences to build, shape and inform the adoption practices that were being created on our behalf. Times are changing, and this book you are holding proves that.

I am excited to invite you into Jacob's personal adoption journey. There are aspects of Jacob's story that are personal to him and then there are themes of his story that are mirrored in all our expeditions toward a more complete understanding of ourselves. Join Jacob on his journey of self-discovery from questioning who he is to where he belongs, a path so many of us have traveled, adopted or not. By reading this book you are putting yourself in the presence of someone who is creating space for normalizing language and experiences in order to ensure people (adoptees) do not feel isolated. I am so grateful to Jacob for his willingness to be vulnerable and share his adventure with us all.

Sincerely,
Astrid Castro

INTRODUCTION

PEOPLE YOUNG AND OLD SAT CHATTING WHILE seated at round tables with fine beige tablecloths at an intimate, family-owned Italian restaurant one evening. The collective tinkling of silverware and low buzz of conversations was accompanied by scents of garlic, tomatoes and mozzarella. Even in the dim lighting, it was obvious all the guests at the tables were white. All except for two young people: a boy and a girl. Upon first glance, the boy was black and maintained an afro. The girl was lighter in complexion but still obviously not of complete European descent. A few other adults sat at the same table along with an elderly couple who smiled for pictures and made light conversation with those stopping by the table to congratulate them on their anniversary.

The boy suddenly got up from his seat and wandered to the table where guests could serve themselves red fruit punch. He thoughtfully poured four cups and began carrying them back to his table to share. An older gentleman in an olive-green suit with spotty facial hair snapped his fingers at the boy and called to him quickly, "when you're finished with that table you can bring some punch over here as well." Dumbfounded, the seventh-grade boy checked to see if the man was in a wheelchair or if crutches were nearby. Maybe that would explain the condescending tone and justify why he could not get his own punch. No wheelchair. No crutches either. "Well, I think you can get it yourself", the boy replied, more as a matter of fact as opposed to an arrogant display of defiance. The man crossed his arms across his chest and moved to scold the boy, but the seventh-grader was already back at the table distributing the punch...

...to his family. That seventh-grader was me. I was at the restaurant for the same reason the old man was: to celebrate my grandparents' fiftieth wedding anniversary. Out of the corner of my eye I caught a glimpse of some of the waiting staff in one of the back rooms. There were two black faces. The old man mistook me for one of the bus boys, even though the only person in the building with an afro was me.

It did not seem appropriate to tell my parents what happened at the restaurant in the same way I never felt comfortable talking to them about the stares we would get whenever we were out in public together. Nor did it feel proper to talk to them about feeling out of place at family gatherings as their/our relatives discussed which new baby resembled whom in the family. Whenever those conversations surfaced, I found myself wanting to be at home in my bed. Or anywhere for that matter. The question that began to emerge was something to the effect of: did I belong? If so, how or why? It is in that spirit of tireless introspection that I decided to write this memoir.

I offer my experiences not as a guide, but certainly as an opportunity to dive headfirst into productive reflection for everyone involved in the adoption triad – biological parents, adoptive parents and adoptees. By no means do I consider myself an expert on adoption. I am actually quite ignorant to the body of academic literature surrounding the topic. I am, however, an expert on the lived experiences that directed me to this moment.

It is also important to note that my target audience extends beyond those with a direct or indirect connection to adoption or adoptees. This memoir is intended to be a gateway to sustained conversations and debates about the very notion of belonging – however the reader wishes to interpret that concept. Regardless of our individual or collective life experiences, we all yearn to belong to something. Maybe we wish to belong to a team. Perhaps we nurse a desire to belong to a partnership. A new department at work. An annual membership. A country. A city. A family.

The details of my own story possess elements related to a substantial array of experiences. And that is sort of the point. We *all* possess that. It is up to us to embrace what connects us, to embrace what brings us together and even more so now as many around the world elect to divide us.

As you embark on some of the most intimate aspects of my life, dear reader, you will laugh. You might cry. You will be angered. Ultimately, it is my sincere hope you will be moved to discuss how exactly *you* belong. How you choose to belong.

Because, if we are honest, it is indeed a choice.

MAP OF COLOMBIA
AND THE CITY OF CALI
POINTS OF INTEREST RELEVANT TO THE STORY
Guaduales
Hotel
Stein Colonial
San Antonio
San Fernando
Hospital
Universitario
del Valle
Canchas
Panamericanas
Futbol
Decepaz
Mojica
Ciudad
Córdoba
Cartagena
Medellin
Bogotá
Cali
Popayán
Tumaco
Pasto
Centro De
Adopción Chiquitines

* * *

I am in a particularly pensive mood. It is approaching six o'clock on a crisp October afternoon in 2002 and dark clouds are slowly rolling in above the jagged ensemble of dark green trees. Walking back to my dorm and still caked in sweat from soccer practice, light rain drops scatter themselves on the paved path in front of me and my phone rings. On the other end is my good friend Daniela's mom Gloria, asking what I will do in December.

"I'm going to Maui with my family again." I reply, unsure of what she is getting at.

"Oh, that's too bad. You won't be able to come with us to Colombia then."

Immediately I demand an explanation, almost appalled at my own sudden lack of manners. Gloria just chuckles and repeatedly instructs me to calm down. Once I gain my composure, she tells me how she and Daniela are traveling to Colombia for a few weeks at the end of the year to visit family. Gloria was born and raised in Colombia. She maintains a strong connection to her extended family there. I will be a welcomed guest.

There is a slight pause on the other end of the phone and almost simultaneously the first crack of thunder invades the small campus. At this point I can care less when the rain comes. It will not matter at all. "Count me in!" I yelp at Gloria. I assure her I will speak with my parents about potentially skipping the family trip for a different family trip. She is still giggling to herself and offers one more suggestion before wishing me a pleasant evening: "be sure to start the process to get your passport as soon as possible."

My life is at a pivotal moment. I just turned eighteen only six months ago and am beginning to navigate collegiate life. It feels like I am just beginning to piece together who I am. I am wrestling with questions surrounding my ethnic identity, playing collegiate soccer, learning about U.S. foreign policy for the first time only a year after the tragic events of September eleventh and what all of it means for the person I will develop into. That process of constructing one's own identity is not something I have given much thought to at all. Traveling to Colombia has the potential to completely change that.

Returning to my country of origin after being adopted from there eighteen years ago also represents a list of challenging questions: will I feel like I belong in Colombia? What if the answer to that question is 'no'? Or what if I find out I do not want to belong at all? Conversely, what would happen if I like it better there than in the U.S.? Will I offend my parents? What will I see that will inspire me? What will I hear that will bring me to tears? Who will I meet and how will we change each other's lives?

I feel slightly nauseous as I close the door behind me in my dorm. My head is heavy with these questions. I have studied the country a lot these past few years, mostly via this growing phenomenon called the internet. But the observations I made and conclusions I arrived at are things I have been able to control. Going there? I will be entirely at the mercy of those around me and the circumstances they choose to expose me to. I will not have any control. There is something both alarming and liberating about that.

As I pick up the phone again to call my parents, I am reminded of a promise they made to me when I was little. They ran out of answers long ago about my life before adoption but insisted they would support me in my first trip back to Colombia if I ever wanted to see it.

That time is now.

I am already smiling as I tap the 'call' button.

* * *

CHAPTER 1

Yellow, Blue and Red Bliss

I FELT MY SOCKS DAMPEN WITH ANXIOUS SWEAT AS our plane descended from the sun kissed clouds. My breathing rapidly accelerated, and I scrambled to clear a thin layer of condensation that collected on the plane window, obstructing my view of what unfolded below.

The sprawling metropolis of Bogotá awaited us with its mountains acting as outstretched arms welcoming us home after a prolonged absence. Indeed, the last time I set foot in Colombia was shortly after the finalization of my adoption process and my new mother and grandmother sat eagerly beside me on a plane bound for Miami, and ultimately, Seattle.

I could not take my face away from the window as we glided over vast fields of foliage composed of shades of greens and browns, heading toward the runway. Despite the significance of the moment, I remained calm. That series of moments before landing in a new place never ceases to evoke anticipation and, for me on this particular occasion, unabashed awe.

We touched down to a series of familiar sounds and intermittent halting as the pilots applied the brakes and landing gear. "*Damas y caballeros, bienvenidos a Bogotá, Colombia*[1]." Once inside the dimly lit corridor of El Dorado National Airport, Daniela and Gloria hurried to use the bathroom, leaving me to push and pull our luggage through the immigration line on my own. They were very clear with their instructions, "Do NOT let anyone in front of us. We'll be right back." I dismissed their anxiety as overly cautious and it took all of one minute before I was trampled by a stampede of impatient Colombian mothers and *abuelas*, pushing past me with hisses and sighs, muttering phrases in hurried Spanish I could not decipher. I let nearly fifteen people go ahead of me. Shortly thereafter my travel companions returned with disappointed looks on their faces. Their eyes darted in front of us and then, almost simultaneously, they said in unison shaking their heads, "we told you so", and we continued to wait.

In late 2002, the airport in Bogotá was not at all what it is today. It was relatively small, which surprised and somewhat disappointed me. I expected the largest city in the country to have an impressive airport that mirrored the city's overbearing nature.

Gloria, Daniela and I sipped on coffee as we sat in the busy terminal, watching and wondering where people were coming from and heading to. Looking around at other travelers in the terminal I noticed a group of young men wearing matching green and white sports uniforms. Upon closer observation, I realized it was arguably the best soccer team in the country at that time: Atlético Nacional from Medellín. One of their players, a

1 Ladies and gentlemen, welcome to Bogotá, Colombia

midfielder named Freddy Grisales, had played for the Colombian national team a year earlier and won the South American championship game. He was considered one of the best players in the country at that time; and there he sat listening to music and flirting with eager female fans only a few meters away from me. My ability to speak Spanish was virtually non-existent at the time, but I decided to approach him and ask for a picture. I was an eighteen-year-old soccer enthusiast, and this was my first interaction with anyone in my first country. It felt cool to be in that moment. Freddy was relaxed, clearly accustomed to his freshly acquired national fame. The brief interaction concluded with a firm handshake, a smile and "*disfrute Colombia*[2]."

Our connecting destination was the smaller city of Pereira, the proud heart of the coffee-growing region tucked away between mountains with a year-long loyalty to a perfect green. The turbulence on the flight from Bogotá seemed to trace the uneven tips of the mountains below us for the entirety of the forty-minute trip and, upon landing, the plane erupted with applause and cheers of elation. I was astounded, having never witnessed such a reaction for a plane landing, but as I came to learn, it was one of a variety of ways in which Colombians say 'gracias' and celebrate even the most mundane aspects of life.

We were able to get our luggage out relatively quickly and once outside, a massive gathering of people stood behind a gate, waving their arms and whistling in anticipation of the arrival of their loved ones. They cheered and smiled, snapping pictures while holding flowers and hand-written signs. For us, the smiles came from a handful of Daniela and Gloria's extended family members, including cousins, aunts and uncles. I felt immediately

2 Enjoy Colombia

welcomed by their warmth, even as a slight breeze warned of rain. The seven or eight of us piled into a dark blue Willy's Jeep along with all our luggage. I was able to stand on the back bumper, hanging onto whatever I could as we winded through the streets toward one of Daniela's uncle's houses.

The next morning, I caught my first glimpse of the city and of daily urban Colombian life - buses, taxis and motorcycles were everywhere. Their chaotic zigzagging and honking produced a constant buzz to which my acquiescence was inevitable. December light decorations were commonplace in windows, plazas and many parks. Even during that month, the heat in the mountains was a welcome change from the frigid and gray atmosphere of the Pacific Northwest which I was accustomed to.

One of the aspects of the city I appreciated immediately was the way people interacted with each other in the streets. A simple 'hello' evolved into so much more. It became an event, almost an invitation to a playful exchange of words. There is an unspoken and unwritten rule that one must outlast each social interaction by responding with unending pleasantries. For example, a response to "how is your day?" might be something like "all good, and yours?"

"Great! Everything beautiful?!"

"Oh yes, very good!"

"Cool."

"And for you?"

"Yes, my king."

"Have a great day."

"You too!"

"Thanks, see you later."

"Hopefully!"

Of course, not all interactions will follow this bubbly script, but the general expectation was that each greeting demanded and deserved to be genuinely responded to.

Body language was another social aspect I noticed that was different. People were incredibly expressive with their hands and used them as they spoke like an orchestral conductor guiding tone and pitch. And people smiled. They smiled almost everywhere I looked; patrons smiled across the street at the bakery, the taxi driver beamed as he helped his elderly client out of his bright yellow cab and two young lovers exchanged smiles and giggled as they sat together on a bench in the shade of the plaza nearby. These social norms intrigued me and almost as soon as I began to assimilate to them, a frustrating realization befell me: I could not communicate in Spanish.

Fortunately, the accent in the Pereira area is not insurmountable to understand, I just needed to get comfortable repeating "*puede hablar más despacio, por favor*[3]*?*" I stumbled around new vocabulary words, which included a whole arsenal of profanity I made sure to silently practice to myself more often than was necessary. The verbs and their layers of confusing conjugations fiercely overwhelmed me, not unlike the ants which frequently invaded my shoes in the night. My pronunciation was horrible. I could not roll my R's and my vowels remained drawn-out in my North American accent.

As I became more familiar with Gloria and Daniela's family, they felt more comfortable making jokes both around me and at my expense; many outlandish and others subtle, but none more perfect than the episode I fell victim to on our brief trip down to Cali.

---

3 Can you speak slower, please?

We arranged for a white and blue minivan to shuttle us from Pereira south through the lush Valle del Cauca department and on to its sprawling capital and my birth city: Santiago de Cali. Cali for short. Foolishly, I only packed enough clothes for two days since we did not determine how long we would be visiting. Our shuttle driver arrived on-time outside Gloria's brother's house and after piling in, we were on our way. I sat in the front and Gloria, Daniela and one of Daniela's cousins, Juan Diego, all sat in the back. The driver, slightly heavy set, boisterous yet warm, played salsa music on the radio. With his thick mustache and short black hair, he resembled a famous Puerto Rican salsa artist named Maelo Ruiz, who continues to enjoy almost unrivaled popularity in Colombia. He tapped his fingers on the steering wheel as he drove and I tried desperately to understand the conversation being had between him and my companions. Gloria and Juan Diego took turns interpreting so Daniela and I could participate. The drive from Pereira to Cali takes approximately three hours so it was a nice opportunity to get to know our driver. They explained to him that it was my first time in Colombia since birth. He asked if I liked what I had seen and, without thinking twice, my answer was an enthusiastic "*sí*!"

The crisp air of the mountainous Risaralda department gave way to the sweltering humidity of the Valle del Cauca. The air conditioning in the minivan seemed more of an obsolete distraction than a combatant in an effort to reduce my surging sweat. Someone warned me against wearing jeans on this ride—and I paid severely for not heeding their advice. My jeans adhered to my thighs and calves, almost mocking me for my foolish decision. Juan Diego and the driver insisted it would be good training for arriving in Cali, at this point roughly an hour away.

We made a pit stop in the small town of Andalucía. I momentarily escaped the puddle of sweat that my seat had become and changed into a pair of swim shorts before returning to the van. Small towns along the Pan-American highway like the one we were in usually had at least one open-air restaurant, a few bathroom stalls and small shops with souvenirs and candies for sale. I got the impression early on that Colombians were extreme sweets enthusiasts and this particular stop further confirmed this. There were different kinds of cookies, sweet breads, gums, lollypops and a small variety of North American candies in the shops.

Back in the minivan, Gloria and Juan Diego passed around a white and red plastic jar filled with small cookies called *beso de novia*. They had a unique texture, almost like a combination of oatmeal cookies and cotton candy. It was crunchy at first and melted as I chewed. Truly unique but too sweet for my taste. Daniela motioned that I should try *gelatina*. I did not trust the look of it from the beginning. The *gelatinas* in this particular town were dark, rectangular in shape and sticky to the touch. They smelled a bit like black licorice, an aroma which had earned my repugnance sometime during childhood. I held it between my fingers, inspecting it. I was stalling and Daniela sniffed it out quickly: "just take a bite, you pansy!" Down it went, with all its slimy glory despite my immediate apprehension. I used some of the *beso de novia* cookies to chase it down as Gloria handed me the paper package the gelatinas had come in. She said I could read the ingredients to put my mind at ease and offered to translate it for me if there was anything unclear. I read "*azúcar,* sugar"—No problem there. Then "*ano y pata de res*" and I recoiled with disgust. For the monolingual English reader, *ano y pata de res* translates roughly to 'cow anus and hoof'.

There are a few things that happen when you realize you have just swallowed something containing the sphincter of a cow. Perhaps some in this situation would play it cool and calmly ask for more cookies. Others might gag and sprint to the bathroom desperately clutching their toothbrush and paste. I reacted with anger and disbelief, scolding my friends for deceiving me. I hurled the paper packaging back at Gloria and told her to read the ingredients. After a few seconds she playfully passed it to Juan Diego and Daniela as she heartily laughed. Tears formed in her eyes as she wailed. Everyone took turns reading the package, including our driver, and the minivan's windows fogged from the collective expression of glee at my misfortune. I was dumbfounded. How was it funny that I had just eaten cow ass? Then, all at once, they yelled that the bag was faded and actually read "*mano y pata de res*", which changed the meaning completely.

The 'M' had been changed somehow.

Still not ideal to be snacking on a conglomerate of cow hooves, but obviously a significant improvement from anus. My confidence restored, I joined them in laughter.

Light raindrops scattered on the minivan's windshield as our driver triumphantly announced our arrival to Cali. "*Bienvenido a casa,* welcome home", he said, wearing a wide smile and patting me on the shoulder with his free hand. In a way, it was a homecoming, but I felt at odds with calling Cali home. I struggled to justify whether or not I had permission to do so. How could a place I never lived in suddenly be considered a home?

As we drove, banks, grocery stores, parks, bars, homes and hotels shot up around us – some dirty, others impeccable. The streets were bombarded by motorists in multicolored buses, motorcycles and taxis. Vibrant colors were in every direction. Palm trees of various heights, brick buildings, tinted windows, and iron bars on doorways made up the scenery around us. It was similar to Pereira but with a more tropical feel.

Vendors seemed to be on nearly every street corner selling fruits, cell phone minutes and ice cream. One that caught my eye was a man selling ice cream from a push cart, his brown face glistening with sweat in the sunlight. He shouted and smiled at cars passing by and kept a small red cloth in one of his hands which he used to wipe his brow. He wore a Bon-ice bodysuit, that looked plastic from the vantage point of our minivan, with a perfectly-matched baseball cap on his head. I felt sorry for him in that heat. But I learned quickly that in Cali, one can curse the humidity as much as possible but doing so changes nothing. You must embrace it.

Our stay in Cali was going to be brief. The plan was to spend a few days seeing the city and visiting members of the extended Castaño family while also visiting my first official place of residence: Chiquitines Centro de Adopción. Luckily, I had already established a connection with the orphanage and its director at the time, Agatha León. The following is an excerpt from a summary I asked her to write detailing our first email exchanges:

The twenty-sixth of March of 2002, we received an email from Mrs. Angie Ryan of the adoption agency World Association for Children and Parents in the Seattle area of the U.S. She informed us a young man, named Jacob Taylor, was adopted from Chiquitines in 1984 and now wished to contact us. I arrived relatively recently to Chiquitines (contracted in December of 2001) and it seemed like a new and exciting experience, to be in contact with an adopted youth who wanted to know more about his origin and the institution.

We began to correspond via email and in his email, Jacob expressed his interest to visit Chiquitines someday. He seemed very happy and excited to return to Colombia. Eventually, it was established he would visit with a friend and her family (from Pereira and Cali) in December of that same year. He would spend Christmas in Colombia and then return to the U.S. shortly after. He asked me many questions about Chiquitines, the children and of course, he began to ask about his origin. He told me he always wanted to know more about where he was from, something I found to be completely normal. In the messages I responded letting him know that as soon as he was in Cali, he could come visit us and I could show him his adoption documents. We kept a file of all adoptions through our institution.

Jacob always maintained a happy and enthusiastic tone in his emails. I think seeing that excitement, I felt even more inclined to try to help him resolve his questions about his biological family, even though I saw very little information in his documents that could help in that matter. It should be mentioned that there was no information about him or his adoptive family post-adoption. I was intrigued to know more about his adoption experience and about his life in general. I asked him to bring pictures when he came to Cali.

We were able to meet on the seventeenth of December 2002 on his first visit to Colombia. Jacob arrived with his friend Daniela, her mother Gloria and a handful of their family members. He seemed like a nice young man and very happy to be here. He brought a suitcase full of candy for all the children, something that is not normal with these types of visits. These little things gave me a positive image of Jacob and his nobleness as well as thoughtful nature.

Returning to the orphanage for the first time produced a strange anxiety in me. I was neither ecstatic nor frightened, rather my feelings oscillated between the two. The mere idea of being in the same physical space with young children who might make the same journey back someday and ask the same questions as I thrust me into a deep feeling of solidarity with them.

My heart raced as we sat in the waiting room of the orphanage for Agatha. We were a medium-sized party of myself, Daniela, Gloria, two of Gloria's brothers (Carlos and Jorge) and two of Jorge's children, Jorge Luis and Marcela. Finally, the wooden door swung open and a thin woman appeared wearing a gentle smile and short gray hair. Agatha forewent typical Colombian social pleasantries and spoke with a firm and direct yet excited tone as she approached and asked, "*y dónde está Jake*? Where is Jake?" It was not for a lack of respect to the others; it was simply because she was excited to finally meet me after so many email exchanges. I rose my hand and she instantaneously hugged me and motioned for me to follow her toward her spacious office with a dark floor. We both took seats and I inched closer to the round glass table. "Welcome to Cali! We are happy you are with us today. How has your trip been so far?" We talked for a few minutes, mostly about details we had already exchanged in our email correspondence and then she opened a vanilla folder resting on the table. "This is your adoption file. I can translate the main points and you can ask me questions but then you will need to take some copies with you for more information."

The pile of documents lying on the table intrigued me. Many years earlier I was told finding them would be an insurmountable feat. And yet, there they were. That moment remains etched in my mind to this day. I wondered if I would feel disappointed or hopeful after reading them. What new pieces of information would surface? Would they lead me to my biological family? Was such a thing possible or was it foolish to dream of such things?

As we began to read, Agatha translated slowly and deliberately, her eyes never straying from the weathered pages. It was clear this had become an important endeavor for her as well. I will be forever grateful to her for her kindness, patience and willingness to help. Pausing, she rotated the page to face me so that I could read along with her, and using her index finger, she pointed to a sentence and slowly said, "it states that since the third month of pregnancy Ms. Mosquera decided to give the baby in adoption." I remained calm. Nothing about the information shocked or saddened me. After all, over the entirety of my life, I had plenty of time to consider many possibilities for my relinquishment.

The essential summary of the documents was this:

María Deisy Mosquera Castillo was thirty-years old when she gave birth to me via C-section in the region's most important hospital called Hospital Departamental Universitario del Valle, in the city of Cali. She lived in a small apartment in the Mariano Ramos neighborhood at the time, and already had a five-year-old son. She was born in the small coastal city of Tumaco, close to the border with Ecuador. There was no name provided or additional information about my biological father. After my relinquishment, one of the local newspapers called El Diario ran a small ad with my picture asking if anyone had information about my family. It was a last-minute effort to locate family members before moving forward with the adoption process. Looking back on it, I do not think I had enough time that day to process the realization that I had an older brother somewhere. I only allowed myself a moment to consider what he might be like before it was time to meet the children at Chiquitines.

We returned to the waiting room and, with a swift motion of her hand and light smile, Agatha escorted me and my small entourage toward the cafeteria of the orphanage where sounds of children emanated. The large wooden cafeteria door opened, and we entered a room full of young children whose eyes immediately shifted towards us as their chatter reduced to a collective silence. Then, all of a sudden as if it had been rehearsed, they erupted with, "*Buenas tardes*!" and waved enthusiastically. Agatha asked that the students settle down and proceeded to introduce me and my friends. I stood there with my dark green suitcase full of candy as Agatha introduced me as Alfonso Mosquera – a name I had only just heard for the first time – the one from my adoption documents. She explained to the children that it was my first time back to Colombia and that I wanted to spend time with them and share some candy I brought from the U.S. The children vied for us to visit their tiny, white plastic tables. "*Alfonso, ven aquí*! Alfonso, come here!" "*No, por aquí*! No, over here!" My friends and I spread out and walked slowly around the brick-floor room distributing candies as we went. In a frenzy, we posed for pictures and exchanged hugs, smiles, and high-fives with all of the children in attendance.

They comprised the diverse range of ethnicities found in the country, and yet they all seemed united as one. There did not appear to be division based on skin color as there had been outside of Chiquitines' walls in the increasingly segregated Cali. I concluded that their shared experience demanded sustained camaraderie. As I passed out candy it hit me; these children were old enough to speak, run, dance, fight, swim and play and most of them would remember being there.

Their first memories would be waiting for a family.

I never endured such brutal uncertainty. Of course their welcoming "*buenas tardes*" was rehearsed! Everyone who came through that door could be a potential adoptive family! How many times had they watched a smiling white couple from the U.S., Europe or Australia visit the orphanage speaking a language they could not understand and walk out holding a black or brown Colombian baby in their arms, never to be seen again? What did I represent to them? I glanced downward and my eyes connected with those of a young black boy with short hair. His eyes were bright and his light blue t-shirt with dark trim clung to his thin frame. Realizing I had caught him staring, he hurriedly buried his bashful face in his palms and giggled hysterically.

Our time with the kids came to an end after my suitcase was emptied of its contents and it was time for them to resume their daily activities. Everyone enjoyed themselves tremendously and that was part of what I struggled with most as I walked out of that cafeteria - I did not want to leave. I wanted to stay with the children as long as possible. I thought perhaps they could teach me to speak a handful of phrases in Spanish or I could teach English to them. Or I could simply be present for them and listen. I could have stayed all afternoon and night just listening to them. Their stories must have been so traumatic. After all, they were in a state-sponsored facility separated from their biological families. I took my time walking back to the lobby where everyone waited, contemplating all the visit represented for me and for the children. I felt a palpable realization overcome me and it took seeing tears stream down Daniela's face for me to fully articulate what it was.

"You're so lucky!" she exclaimed as salt from her tears dried on her face. At the sight of her tears, I began to sob and tried to dry my face in the lobby bathroom with a small white towel. Seeing her cry felt like a kind of authorization for me to do the same; it was alright to give in to the weight of the moment. These children knew they were waiting for a family - someone to call *mamá* and *papá*. My first memories were so different. A wave of guilt washed over me, even though I recognized I was not at fault. It was the first time in my life in which I thoroughly analyzed, in the moment, the reason why I wept. Why had I been spared this grueling experience? What happened to the other children in the orphanage when I was there? Where in the world were they? Were they alright? I felt culpable and deeply saddened by the prospect of older children watching me be taken away by smiling white faces, wondering when it would be their turn, if ever. What unbearably penetrating grief!

As we drove away from Chiquitines that cloudy afternoon, I recall the sensation of my body struggling to regain bearings, akin to the way one sways for a time after arriving back on land having been out to sea. I was taken hostage by the incessant, lingering rocking. Perhaps it comes as no surprise that I do not remember any details about our drive back into the city. I was both physically and emotionally drained. My head pounded, my palms and back were caked with salty sweat. My mouth was dry, and my eyes stung. I am sure we talked during the ride back. I am sure there was some kind of social gathering that evening with Daniela and Gloria's family. Yet, none of it has earned a place in my memory. My mind was fixed on those children. It would take me the drive back north to Pereira, along with the flights back to Washington state to regain mental clarity.

The weeks and months to come after my visit would challenge me to begin to answer the question, "who was I?"

CHAPTER 2

Question Marks

ONCE BACK IN WASHINGTON STATE, MIRRORS AND A public sea of predominately white faces constantly reminded me I was different from others. One of the results of getting a small taste of Colombia and being back in the U.S. was yearning for a social group that more closely resembled the ethnic diversity I saw all around me during my visit. Was it possible to create something similar in the greater Seattle area? Nowhere was it more apparent that I was different than when I would visit with my parents.

Perhaps because of my heightened awareness about my developing concept of ethnicity, being out in public with my parents began to cause a quiet consternation in me. People were confused and curious as to why a young black man would be dining with a white couple considerably older than he was. My parents never seemed to notice the stares or occasional confused bits of laughter. I noticed all of them. Yet I never mentioned anything to my parents. Without ever fully articulating any profound sentiment regarding race or ethnicity, it was obvious to me they were content to exist in a color-blind world. Conversations regarding these topics were virtually non-existent in our home growing up and that extended into my first few years of adulthood. I do not want to give the impression they did not care about these issues, nor do I find it appropriate to label them as ill-intentioned parents. Certainly, nothing could be further from the truth. However, for reasons I will never fully comprehend, I think it is fair to claim they have always clung to a certain level of reluctance regarding the topics of ethnicity and privilege. My assumption is this was a result of there simply not being an abundance of resources available both before and after they adopted my sister and me, nor did they have any friends with similar experiences regarding adopting children from other countries. In addition, I think they genuinely find it uncomfortable to engage in those kinds of discussions. I have come to understand this reality and harbor no ill-tempered thoughts toward them. They simply have never *needed* to consider their ethnicity as it relates to their sense of self, as it relates to access and privilege in the same ways I have. In that regard, we have developed different ways to ponder who we are.

Our relationship and, frankly, lack of conversations regarding these topics only stoked the flames of curiosity within me and I was inspired to seek out more answers about who I was. Equally important to me was a quest to understand how others perceived me. The first step in that process came while beginning to piece together my academic future.

For enrollment at Tacoma Community College (TCC), I needed to fill out paperwork detailing my identity. The familiar bubbles requesting I select an ethnicity appeared, somehow more perplexing and intimidating than the multiple previous times throughout my life because of my recent experiences in Colombia. The instructions were clear: PLEASE SELECT ONE. The 'please' fascinated me because it implied an attempt to be polite while still demanding a single response. But, what about those of us who feel a tremendous pull to check two boxes? Three? I chose the option for 'non-white Hispanic' but felt it did not fully express who I was, especially since I knew that people did not immediately perceive me to be part of the Hispanic group. The average person seeing me in my car or at the bank, for example, would assume I ought to fill in the African American box and selecting anything else would, at best, be met with prolonged confusion.

The logical conclusion was to tackle the formidable question head-on: am I black? If the answer was to be "yes", then I needed and wanted to know how and why. Similarly, if the answer was "no", I also wanted to dissect why. I deeply wanted to know what made a person black aside from the color of their skin. It made sense to take the question to my black friends in order to get their perspective on the matter. There was just one small problem: I did not have any black friends! I *was* the token black friend in my social circles during those years. I was the token black friend while having no experience living with black families, no experience dating black women, no experience living in predominately black neighborhoods and no experience learning about black history (in the U.S. or internationally) aside from the half page about Martin Luther King Jr and the Civil Rights Movement in my history text books. The task before me was to determine what the concept of self meant for me and my particular set of experiences.

The American philosopher, George Herbert Mead, was one of the first to articulate the very complex idea of what constitutes the self. I am unable to discuss his ideas and academic or philosophical contributions at length, but I do think the following helps to unpack what I was starting to grapple with in the chase to answer my question about being black:

> The self is something which has a development; it is not initially there, at birth, but arises in the process of social experience and activity, that is, develops in the given individual as a result of his relations to that process as a whole and to other individuals within that process[4].

To agree with Mead, my views surrounding my ethnicity (or ethnicities) depended greatly on how I felt I was perceived by others. As I mentioned, others saw me in public as African American, yet I wanted to find a way to belong to the Hispanic community too. I yearned for the best of both worlds. What constituted my *self* was (and remains) inextricably bound to how others identify me, and vice versa. If others see me as black, then, in a way, I am black, regardless of how much I wish to confirm or deny it. Even if these concepts were beginning to make logical sense to me, others had conflicting ideas of who I was.

At TCC, I sought out the Black Student Union only to hear from one of the leaders that I had not passed the test: "Nah bro, you ain't even that black." That was my first and last interaction with that particular student organization. What did "that black" even mean? What would it look like to change this leader's perspective? Who or what held that power?

---

4 George Herbert Mead, "The Social Self", Journal of Philosophy, Psychology and Scientific Methods 10, 1913: 374-380.

The following week I walked nervously into the Latino Student Alliance introductory meeting and while initially my presence was met with visible skepticism by the mostly Mexican American and Puerto Rican leaders, after a few weeks I was elected Vice President. What did that mean? I wondered if it suggested I was more accepted by Hispanic communities than black communities in general or exclusively at TCC.

During that time, I experienced another bewildering incident that contributed to the development of my concept of self and ethnicity. A group of long-term friends and I parted ways. The five of us met during elementary school on a soccer team. As the years rolled on, we developed a friendship both on and off athletic fields which included baseball, track and soccer. Our families became relatively close as we embarked on the journey to navigate the perils of puberty. We trusted each other and became almost inseparable, even as two from our group left us for a private high school in the neighboring city of Tacoma. We remained united and as I began to understand my blackness in my early twenties, something shocking happened.

One evening we were out enjoying beers, most likely engaged in a conversation about women or soccer (they were the only topics we thought we knew anything about), when one of them said, "hey reggin, pass me another beer." There was music playing and I did not hear exactly what was said, but my friend was looking directly at me when he said it, so I tossed him a beer and we continued on with our night.

During another evening, we were at another bar engaging in the same activities, and again, this word was used repeatedly in conversation. Then I heard another unfamiliar word: "hey nooc, when are we going to play soccer again?", one of them asked gleefully. On this occasion we were at my parents' house, standing outside in the driveway after kicking the soccer ball around. By this point, these strange words seeped into nearly all of our interactions and I was beyond curious as to what they meant. So, I asked one of them, who at the time, I considered to be my best friend. I will never forget how he looked first at the ground, as if having an internal debate whether or not to tell me, his face turning pale. "You really don't know?" he murmured. "No idea, man." I replied while waiting, by then a bit concerned. He let out a sigh like I had never seen from him before. It was a sunny day, but I felt cold with dread before he said quickly, "just spell the words backwards and it'll make sense." Spelled backwards, the words that had been used were 'nigger' and 'coon'. I was shocked.

My childhood friends took the time to mask not one but two racial slurs and use them on me on multiple occasions. Their thoughtless behavior was inexcusable and resulted in the demise of our friendship built over the course of a little more than a decade. I felt they did not deserve a place in my life anymore having repeatedly referred to me in this way with smiles on their faces – they did it in bars, on fields, in restaurants and, that day, at the house I grew up in. I could not fathom a greater form of disrespect. Immediately, I cast them aside, all four of them; and their families as well, which hurt deeply because I had grown to love them. In my mind, the only decision that made sense was to forget about them and focus on the people in my life who were not disrespectful to me and work on developing a richer understanding of Colombia and my relationship to it.

That spring, I made researching Colombian culture more of a priority. The Spanish I was learning sporadically was a fusion of Mexican, Peruvian, Puerto Rican and Honduran accents and slang by virtue of who I was playing soccer and socializing with. I had no formal instruction, but I was listening to Colombian pop music on a weekly basis and maintained an emerging curiosity for the politics of the country as well. I did not have any friends or acquaintances born and raised in the country nor did I have my current network of fellow Colombian adoptees. Besides my good friend Daniela and her mom Gloria, I did not have an outlet to enquire about the country. Imagine my excitement upon learning about a viewing party at a bar in Seattle to watch the Colombian national soccer team begin their World Cup qualifying campaign.

I arrived early and alone that night, proudly wearing my bright yellow Colombian soccer jersey. Little by little people arrived - couples, families and groups of friends. There were approximately forty people packed into the tight space in the bar. The atmosphere was jubilant, even after the first goal was scored by the opponent (either Peru or Venezuela).

At the bar I ordered another mojito (generally my cocktail of choice) and someone asked me a question. I smiled lightly, shrugged and responded I did not speak Spanish. "Then why are you here?", demanded my interlocutor, his tone immediately territorial. I proceeded to tell him I was adopted from Colombia and I played soccer all my life, so it made sense to be watching the game. Perhaps I expected what he said next: "ah ok but you're not *really* Colombian then." He patted me on the shoulder, smiled one of those toothless masks of pity people too often perform and disappeared into the sea of yellow shirts with his beer. The game ended 0-1.

Of course, there was a considerable degree of truth behind what the man in the bar said. I was raised in the damp Pacific Northwest corner of the U.S., far from the humid chaos of my native city, Cali. I did not speak Spanish; I had only been in the country for three blissful weeks and possessed no accurate grasp on the historical, social, economic or political realities of Colombia. My Colombian identity resided exclusively in the sweat of my yellow jersey, my Colombian flag bracelet and the fact that I knew most of the lyrics to Shakira's top hits in Spanish, albeit without knowing what they actually meant.

Nonetheless, I was quick to correct people who spelled the country with an infuriating 'u', quick to fire a witty response to feckless statements about the country's association with drugs and quick to insist there were good people in the country despite the decades of headlines detailing the country's unstoppable carnage. I started to contemplate how I could become more Colombian without living there and without having Colombian friends.

Surprisingly for me, the greater Seattle area is home to a significant Colombian immigrant population. As I set out on a mission to find answers to my questions, I realized there was a growing number of events for the Hispanic community in the city and surrounding cities and towns. I would wear my Colombian soccer jersey to these events in an effort to fish for compatriots. On the occasions that it worked, roughly half the time I was met with more patronizing lectures about how I was not Colombian enough. These discussions often ended with the insistence that I learn Spanish; but, as one older gentleman put it, "*español colombiano, nada de esa mierda que se habla en Argentina*[5]*!*"

5 Colombian Spanish, none of that shit they speak in Argentina!

People seemed confounded when I asked if I could be Colombian without speaking Spanish.

Their responses were varied, some in full support and others in staunch opposition, each expressed with similarly animated bursts of enthusiasm. The task of mastering Colombian Spanish while living in Washington State seemed impossible. It made more sense to me to devote myself to learning about the country's history and contemporary issues with a fervor that approached obsession. I spent countless hours studying Colombia's geography, which national parks were where, the multiple musical genres one could find throughout the country and statistics concerning census data. Quizzing myself on the thirty-two departments (similar to provinces), their capital cities and even their individual flags became routine as did comparing and analyzing the variety of regional accents.

In my almost frantic pursuit of becoming an expert on Colombia, yet another question emerged: should my allegiance lie with Colombia or with the U.S.? Was it even appropriate to consider adopting and maintaining loyalties or was it enough to simply be and embrace both simultaneously? A blind nationalism began to materialize within me, which inevitably represented an unforeseen conundrum for those around me, since I had never been particularly patriotic - not even after the tragedies that unfolded on the morning of September eleventh, 2001.

I almost sought out opportunities to lecture people on Colombia's past and present on a variety of topics including pop culture, history, the armed conflict, popular tourist destinations and culinary expressions. Just saying the word 'Colombia' aloud provided me with certain pleasure. By my own standards, certainly nobody else's, I achieved Colombia expert status in those few short months. As to whether or not I should have a stronger allegiance toward one country or the other, I felt like if the two countries were in a foot race, Colombia would win by a centimeter simply because I happened to be born there. At that time in particular, my feelings of belonging were skewed at best. One could argue they were stronger for Colombia because Colombia represented the unknown. The exotic. Mine without truly or fully being mine. Home without having ever been a home. My nationality, without having ever possessed a Colombian passport. Yet, as I discovered in my research, the Colombian constitution determined anyone born in the country was a citizen and had the right to that citizenship for life until that person decided otherwise. This was all the justification I needed, and it became my most potent weapon against the Colombian immigrants suggesting I could never achieve their level of belonging.

So, was I black? Colombian? Was there a way to be both and feel confident owning those two identities? If identifying as both, it felt important to choose which *kind* of black to identify with—North American or South American. I did not have anyone to instruct me whether or not there was a correct answer. Even though these thoughts confused me, I knew I wanted to claim my blackness. There was a certain allure to being able to say I was black, yet I could not express exactly why. Maybe my classes would help?

My favorite class at the community college was an introduction to anthropology taught by the passionate professor Elizabeth Fortenbery. She was a brilliant orator with a sharp wit and explained things in a way that made immediate sense. The classes' exploration of kinship fascinated me as did the lessons regarding linguistics. It was impossible to resist throwing both subjects together and thinking about my biological family in Colombia. If I were to ever meet them, what would we have in common? Would our biological bond suffice for us to construct a sustainable relationship or were the forces of nurture destined to divide us? Which linguistic differences would I discover while getting acquainted with them? What kinds of questions or tensions would arise as a result of our inevitably dissimilar socio-economic status? Would they resent me and my privilege? Would I resent their authentic Colombian experiences and compare them with my tireless pursuit of my own? The thought of searching for my biological family to unravel the answers to these questions gnawed at me fiercely.

And then, one sunny afternoon, I received a phone call from Daniela. "Hey, so I have this crazy idea. My cousin Lucía in Colombia is looking for roommates. What do you say we move down there in August and live with her for a while?"

I was a self-proclaimed Colombia expert, generally bored with my restaurant jobs and prerequisite courses to get to who-knew-what and I was more than ready for a change of scenery.

The decision to move to Colombia took a matter of seconds – "I'm in."

CHAPTER 3

The Taxi Ride

BY COLOMBIAN STANDARDS, THE HOUSE DANIELA, Lucía and I were living in was undeniably upper middle class, cushioned comfortably away in one of the more affluent neighborhoods of the western section of the city, called San Fernando. The house coexisted tightly between two others atop a street on a hill just a block and half from the well-known *Siete esquinas de Cali*, which proudly boasted some of the best hot dogs in the region. It was a unique cemented texture with a dark green trim. There was a large balcony, big enough to host a dance party or a barbecue, which we would experiment with two months later. The door was a matching dark green and was made of thick steel. Once open, one could see how expansive the space was. The dining room extended to a living room, next was the small TV room, although it was more of a breezeway since there were no doors for it. Adjacent to that was the long and narrow kitchen. There were two bedrooms next with a bathroom across the hallway. Then came the third bedroom with its personal small bathroom and the door leading outside to a medium-sized patio for drying clothes. It was too big for just the three of us. However, that did not stop me from claiming the final bedroom and bathroom for myself while Daniela and Lucía could share the other bathroom. The bathroom promised to be a difficult adjustment since the toilet, shower head and sink all shared the same space. In theory, I would be able to shower while sitting on the toilet and using the sink to brush my teeth, for example.

Coming from Pacific Northwest summer heat to Cali humidity was less of an adjustment than arriving during the North American winter like my previous trip. Being back in Colombia after two years to process that first time felt good on many levels and I was excited to see what the next few months would unveil for us. It must be made clear that this excitement did not equate to any sort of expectations. I was solely focused on improving my Spanish skills the best I could and was mentally prepared to do everything possible to make that happen.

The moment demanded a certain level of self-examination I admit I was not fully prepared for. It had been a grueling previous few months in preparation for the trip. I felt slightly uneasy about not knowing what my role would be during my time in the country. Aside from learning Spanish to the best of my ability, I had no other real responsibilities to myself or anyone else. That freedom was more than a bit daunting and left me, on many of those first days and nights, scrambling for a sense of purpose. It would mean prioritizing the priorities, which needed to be determined.

Before I left for Colombia, my mom handed me a journal with a leather cover. Her instructions were very clear: "I know you like to write, so I hope you fill it." Indeed, to this day the journal is completely full and, in this chapter, excerpts from those feelings and questions back in 2004 are included. The first of these excerpts is the following after five days of being back in the country:

> *Martes 10 de Agosto*
>
> *Today we walked around the Alameda street market looking for things for our house. After the girls picked out some flowers and paint, we stood there watching an older man, probably in his fifties at least, holding a hand radio with the salsa turned to high volume and dancing. Every time a girl or woman would pass, he would walk toward her to smile or blow her a kiss, all while still dancing.*

There was no way to escape the reality that virtually every neighborhood in Cali was (and remains) deeply devoted to salsa music. The old man and his contagious joy threw me into an existential frenzy: if I could not dance, how would I fit in? How would I make friends? I was well-accustomed to maintaining a busier-than-average social life and it was clear this would be a significant obstacle if I could not dance. Aside from the language, physical literacy with dancing seemed like a worthy pursuit, until just a couple days later, something else surfaced as a potential priority.

> *Jueves 12 de Agosto*
>
> *Woke up today and ate an arepa. Daniela is not feeling well so we have not gone to the currulao festival yet. The girls watched Kill Bill 2. I would have watched but I have not seen the first one yet. So, I*

> *picked up the Cali phone book in hopes of finding a map of the city. After skimming the pages, I did not find a map. I decided to look for people with the Mosquera Castillo names. I found "Adelina", "Carlos", "Dianeth" and "Elizabeth" before stumbling across the "María" section. There was a whole half page of Marías but then I came to something that made me tremble and sweat at the same time: Mosquera C. María D. CL 78 #28E-94 Tel: #436-2364*

My immediate thought was, "could it really be that easy to find my biological mother?" Honestly, feelings about my biological family had not even had a chance to surface yet because I was still adjusting to what it meant to be living in Colombia for the first time. The sole purpose of the trip, at least during those first few days and weeks, was to do my best to learn the language. Aspirations regarding my biological family were, according to me, off limits since I really had no idea how to begin the search and needed to console with others in my social and professional circles, both at home and in Cali. Still, I was completely captive to my own curiosity. Finding that name in the phonebook sent me into a pensive few days.

It had been some time since I had felt the unsettling fire of ambition towards anything. For lack of a better word, I was ecstatic about the prospect of searching for and finding this woman. A colossal search to find one person out of approximately forty-six million with nothing more than a name seemed completely insane. It seemed ridiculous. It seemed impossible. And yet, it was entirely intriguing. Something about the challenge excited me, even if it implied a major leap into the uncertain and improbable.

"I say you fucking go for it. You really have nothing to lose," Daniela blurted out as she sat across from me sipping her coffee. I was in the beginning stages of trying to reason with myself aloud when she said that. You really have to know Daniela to understand her unique brand of authenticity. What she said was the general consensus among my friends back in the States as well. One friend articulated my sentiments perfectly for me: if I was living in Cali for an extended amount of time, it would be foolish not to try. Moving back to the Seattle area without having attempted anything could have potentially locked me in a perpetual state of regret and I could not afford such a crippling reality. The thought of sitting in a coffee shop looking out at the Northwest rain wondering why I had not done all I could to locate María Deisy and not knowing when I would be back in Colombia again was a truly nauseating prospect. I simply could not let that happen.

While I was certain about how I felt about my decision, there was another element I had not fully considered. How would I find the perfect words to inform my parents? I do not feel I have any authority to speak on behalf of all adoptees. I recognize and respect that fully. However, I doubt many would disagree with me when I say that notifying adoptive parents of a desire to seek out our biological families represents a daunting task to say the least. Think about this for a minute. Many adoptive parents live their lives completely convinced they have saved their children from abject poverty, famine, civil war, a future of limited possibilities for prosperity in all aspects. I think it is unrealistic to reject this notion entirely. My parents certainly never (at least not to me) articulated any sort of patting themselves on the shoulder for having "saved" me from anything or anyone.

They are just not that brand of human. Still, how was I going to tell them? Was the best approach via email so they could have some space and time to process my aspiration or was a direct phone call the more appropriate option? Surely 'best' cannot exist in these circumstances.

> *Lunes 16 de Agosto*
>
> *Tonight, I thought a long time, at least three hours, about my biological mom and what I am going to do. I decided to call my parents because I knew they would have great advice. They told me they were comfortable with everything and they were overwhelmingly supportive. And so, the hunt is on. I will pursue my biological mother and I will find her. If the phone number I found is that of another woman, I will try to get the orphanage to help me since it came up in conversation two years ago. When my Spanish is better, I will compose a letter for her. I will have mom send me some pictures of me, friends, family and make a book for her. I am going to find my biological mother.*

"Well we support whatever decision you want to make regarding your biological family." These were the words on the other end of the phone from my mom as she, like countless times before, calmly dismantled any anxiety I felt. All of my second-guessing and overanalyzing was for naught. I had the support of my parents to go forward with a search and words truly cannot express, in English or Spanish, how much of a boost that was. I knew it was not a comfortable situation for them and I knew that deep down, at their core, the thought made them nervous for the possibility of somehow 'losing' me to my biological family.

The feeling of being caught in the middle of unconditional love from my adoptive parents and the inevitable, profound sense of anguish and shame from my biological mother was (and, if I am honest, continues to be) convoluted at best. I constantly asked myself what the role of guilt was in that space. Was it somehow 'right' to feel guilty for being adopted? Or was it better to feel guilty for wanting to search for my biological family? Perhaps the more difficult question was: which guilt was worse? Why did I feel the need to have a better or worse in the first place?

> *Viernes 8 de Octubre*
>
> *Chiquitines does not have the resources to do a search but Agatha will contact a private investigator in Bogotá to see what can be done. If that fails, I am going to have to take it upon myself to get this started and find answers. It's already been two months. Time to get started.*

As thick raindrops fell on the roof of Chiquitines one afternoon, Agatha pulled me aside and whispered to me that I could contact the private investigator in Bogotá at my earliest convenience. While my confidence with Spanish was climbing more with each week, I still felt more comfortable with writing than speaking, so I sent this person an email. The next day he replied and informed me it would cost $400 USD to begin a search. This seemed extreme to me, especially since there was no guarantee the search would yield any information regarding my biological family. I respectfully declined and as I pressed the 'send' button, my fingers quivered with the realization that for all the determination, all the desire and all the day-dreaming of the possibilities, I had no answers for how to conduct a search. The burning hope I had previously let myself be seduced by was giving way to my own special brand of pragmatic pessimism.

If Chiquitines could not help, if private investigators wanted ridiculous sums of money and if I had no information beyond my biological mother's name and date of birth, how was it remotely realistic to find her or, at the very least, any evidence related to her whereabouts and well-being?

And then, I found myself in the front seat of yet another taxi. Although this time, the taxi ride would be the catalyst for a chain of rather quick life-altering events. It was Thursday October twenty-first of that year, a particularly steamy day. My driver was a man in his mid-forties with a dark shirt, tanned skin and scattered yet short facial hair. Some taxi drivers set the tone for how the ride will go as soon as you get in. If they are open to talking, they will turn down the music. If not, they will simply keep the music or radio on at a volume loud enough to make sure you understand they would prefer to listen to the world beyond the ten, fifteen or twenty-five minutes to be shared with you while driving. However meaningful or meaningless the conversation will be is, in a big way, up to the driver. On that particular afternoon, the music was turned down. There was a considerable amount of traffic along fifth street, one of Cali's main streets connecting the south to the northern neighborhoods. I seized my opportunity for a conversation after seeing a small soccer ball hanging from the rearview mirror supporting the same team I supported, and he was quick to notice my semi-North American accent.

"Where are you from, young man?"

"It's a long story. I was born here but adopted by an American family."

"Oh! Interesting. So, you must be one of those adopted kids who comes back to search for your biological family."

I paused. This was an unnervingly accurate guess. I also guessed it meant he was familiar with other cases. Seconds later, my suspicion was confirmed.

"There are many people like you who come back here from Europe and other places looking for answers about their past. Have you found any information yet?" I went on to explain, as best I could with my limited conjugations, how I was not sure how I could conduct a search. My options were running out and I was doubtful. We came to a red light and the driver took a red cloth from his pocket, slowly wiped the layer of sweat from his forehead, turned to me and said, "why don't you talk to Telepacífico? They have a program called Desaparecidos and maybe they could help." There was no reason not to believe him. He clearly knew what he was talking about and there was just something about him that made me trust his words.

I heard about Telepacífico during my first month in the country. It was a regional television channel offering news, cultural updates and a variety of other programs with a growing number of viewers and aired on the local channel eleven. What I was unaware of was the Desaparecidos program, which sought to help people find missing members of their families or friends, so I pressed the driver for more information. He described how it was a good tool for people searching for their loved ones due to a kidnapping or disappearances. On more than one occasion, he said cheerfully, he saw pictures and stories about mostly European Colombian adoptees searching for their biological families. "We will be passing their headquarters in a few minutes; it is sort of close to where you want to be dropped off. I will show you." I asked to be dropped off at the corner of fifth street and the Parque de las Banderas. The Telepacífico building was located, according to the driver, about a ten-minute walk south from where I was originally planning to get out. We pulled up and he stopped, indicating enthusiastically with his right hand where the main entrance was. Once again giving in to curiosity, I decided to end my trip there. The driver shook my hand, told me good luck with my search and refused to take the money I owed him for the ride. I remember it to be approximately 15,000 pesos (the equivalent of roughly seven dollars at the time) and when I insisted he take it, he laughed and told me to get out of his car. *"Fresco mijo, no te preocupés. Suerte[6]!"*

I yearned for a cold shower and siesta. But this was too good of a lead to pass up. I strolled up to the main entrance, but the lights were off, and it appeared that nobody was inside. I knocked on the glass twice, waited, but nothing. A security guard appeared, and it took only a few seconds of him staring at me to convince me I should leave. On my walk back toward the stadium, Parque de las Banderas and ultimately our house, I decided to return on the following Monday to ask to speak with someone. The weekend was a dizzying blur of playing dominoes, a house dinner party, too much aguardiente, dancing on chairs in a club called Mushiba in the Menga neighborhood and, ultimately, a 5:00a.m. bedtime on Sunday morning.

That Monday I woke up and walked back down to fifth street and the Parque de las Banderas, stopping along the way at a street cafe to eat some *pandebonos* and coffee, along with

6 It's ok 'son', don't worry. Good luck!

some scrambled eggs. From there I made my way further south and back to Telepacífico to try my luck at getting an appointment with someone. This time the door was open but a short man with glasses informed me everyone was too busy because the president was in town, so all journalists and other employees were scrambling to cover his visit. He suggested I return the next day and I was rushed out of the building. As I stepped back out on to fifth street to contemplate where to spend the next couple of hours since we did not have Spanish class that day, it was as if someone had decided to turn on the faucet above the city. Within a few minutes, some of the most persistent and powerful rain I had ever seen was dumping itself on everything. The street immediately transformed from a humid concrete corridor to a brown river, with the occasional aluminum can or plastic utensil floating slowly toward a drain. In the downpour, I sought refuge in a nearby open-air café where I ordered an orange juice and a few empanadas. The rain would surely stop as it often did and then I would be able to resume my trek to wherever I wanted. But the rain continued. I grew impatient and hopped into a taxi to take me home, only a five-minute drive.

Once home I dove into a deep nap and then awoke in the late afternoon to the sound of one of our neighbors blaring vallenato music. I remember thinking there was nothing significant about the day, nothing to really write about, nothing to be inspired by and, for the first time, a sense of boredom overcame me. Little did I know that life was about to be shaken up, forever.

The morning of Tuesday October twenty-sixth, 2004 was just like many others of that year: relaxed, somehow involving eggs and accompanied by the typical carelessness of a twenty-year-old. A few persistent mosquitos greeted me and followed as I brushed my teeth. Daniela stayed home due to a cold, Lucía was at the university and I was out the door, never mentioning where I was going. It made little sense to get them excited for something that would most likely yield no results.

Around 11:00a.m., I arrived at Telepacífico's main entrance with no idea of whom to speak with. A younger man, probably close to my age with pale skin, a light blue shirt and gelled black hair noticed me and asked if he could help with anything.

"Can I speak to someone about the Desaparecidos program?" I asked, trying hard to sound as Colombian as possible. He cocked his head slightly to his left and raised his eyebrows, as if he had detected something odd with my accent.

"Sure. Wait here at this table. I'll be right back."

I sat patiently at a white, bare plastic table, accompanied by two matching chairs, until the young man returned holding some papers and a blue pen. We introduced ourselves and he handed me a sheet to fill out to explain who I was looking for and why. He did not ask any questions or make any small talk at all. His only preoccupation seemed to be his cell phone as he waited for me to write. I wrote that I was born there in Cali, left in the main hospital by my biological mother, placed in Chiquitines and adopted by an American family as a baby. I added the information about my biological mother and mentioned how I was looking for her but did not know what other options to explore.

When I finished, I slid the page across the table for him to read when I finished. His eyes darted back and forth quickly and finally he said in a lower tone, "Oh." He looked up at me, then back at the paper and told me to come with him upstairs to the studio. "You write Spanish well for having been raised in the U.S. There are only a few mistakes here, but it doesn't matter."

I asked why I needed to go with him. The swift laughter he responded with only made me more apprehensive and he blurted, in a no-nonsense sort of way, "*obviamente tienes que contar tu historia a la gente. Tienes una foto de tu madre biológica*[7]*?*" I thought back to the adoption documents Agatha and Chiquitines had provided me a couple years before. No, I told him, I did not possess any picture of María Deisy. He proceeded to tell me that what made the most sense was to interview me about my search and go from there. The problem was, I did not fully understand what he was telling me. The verb he used was '*entrevistar*' and it was a word that had not earned a place on the lists of vocabulary I was studying at the time. "We are going to interview you so you can tell people your story. Does that sound good?" Once he finally broke down the verb, I launched into a tirade of all the reasons why I should not or could not be interviewed. My confidence with Spanish, while significantly elevated compared to my first couple of months in the country, still needed to be developed. I knew I did not have a sufficient grasp of the grammar or vocabulary to be interviewed. Furthermore, my assumption was this would be an interview at the same plastic table from before, or one like it, with a tape recorder. Something simple, in a relaxed setting. "No, no, no" he smiled, sipping his coffee from a red and white plastic cup, "*te vamos a entrevistar en vivo, con luces, cámara y toda la vaina*[8]*!*"

My stomach felt like it was twisting and turning itself into a knot because of the nerves. I was terrified to do a live television interview. Another man, possibly in his mid-forties,

---

7 Obviously, you need to tell people your story. Do you have a picture of your biological mother?

8 We're going to interview you live, with lights, camera and the whole thing!

approached, shook my hand firmly and sputtered off two unintelligible sentences. I asked him to slow down and he repeated himself, explaining how he was going to interview a doctor visiting from Bogotá to discuss local environmental policy. Later, he went on, they would have a quick commercial break before interviewing me about my search.

The studio was spacious. Journalists and video crew members scurried from space to space while on their phones, gelling their hair, adjusting their ties, applying makeup, dropping papers, whispering, shouting and laughing. The air conditioning was relentless and created a frigid atmosphere, yet people still walked and jogged around swiping sweat from their foreheads. I watched from a padded black chair as the doctor from Bogotá fielded the questions in her interview with such collected poise. There was no way I would be able to follow her performance! And to be honest, I cannot remember anything she and the anchor man talked about. The moment was too overwhelming to enjoy what was most likely a lively intellectual conversation. Instead, I focused on my present and past tense verb conjugations and tried to anticipate which verbs I would need to understand and use when my time came.

I must have waited for about forty-five minutes before they took a commercial break and the camera men told me to hurry and sit in the chair next to the desk where the reporter sat, sipping his water and using a small white cloth to wipe his forehead and neck. It was intimidating to be the only one in the building who felt more comfortable speaking English and then there were all the cameras, lights and people to make my palms sweat even more. More and more people came in through the doors as word spread about why I was there. I glanced toward the door and noticed them all whispering, arms folded in anticipation.

A small microphone was clipped to my shirt and I was instructed to look only at the massive camera in front of me and the anchorman. A small water bottle appeared, and a hand quickly touched my head from behind, it was more of a fast pet. Someone was actually concerned with how my short hair would look for television. There was no time to ponder the awkwardness of the entire situation as a lanky man's figure appeared behind the large camera in the darkness and his right hand was held high, with all five fingers completely outstretched. The room grew gradually quieter, the man's hand changed to four fingers, then three, then two, one.

Lights I had not noticed suddenly jumped brightly onto my face. I imagined the sweat making my forehead gleam as the cameras rolled and the anchorman's booming voice announced, "*y estamos de regreso con el joven Jacob Ta...*[9]." After realizing he could not accurately pronounce my last name on his cards before him, he opted for the phonetic version with very Latin American vowels. His speech was quick, and he remembered who was sitting across from him, adjusting the speed of his questioning.

"Tell us, Jacob, what brings you here today?" he bellowed, smiling widely. I fumbled over my words trying to match the speed of his initial question. The only thing that he seemed to understand was when I murmured, "I am searching for my biological mother who probably lives here in Cali." Our conversation touched on all the basics: where in the city I was living, who I was living with, if I enjoyed being in Colombia and then my

9 And we're back with the young man Jacob Ta...

biological mother's complete name, which I repeated a few times. The anchorman gave whoever watching a bit of the context of my story and then, his tone grew quieter and he asked, "And... do you have a phone number for anyone with any information so they can contact you?" I quickly explained I did not have a cell phone and offered the number to our house in San Fernando. "*cinco, cinco, cuatro, quince, cero, ocho es mi número de teléfono en la casa.*"

He shook my hand, turned to face the camera in front of me and declared, "we wish Jacob the best on his important search! Good afternoon and thank you for watching Desaparecidos."

Just like that, the lights dimmed, the cameras made a few clicking sounds and my shoulders relaxed. From beginning to end, we did not pass the ten-minute mark. The anchorman smiled, patted me on the shoulder and stood up, saying "well done, young man" as people came to speak with him. He turned to me once more. "Good luck with your search. Let us know how it goes." With that, he disappeared into the chaotic sea of journalists and air conditioning. Other journalists and employees were in my face immediately to wish me good luck and to retrieve the microphone.

In all honesty, I did not believe anyone would know anything. Cali is a city of roughly three million people and my biological mother's last name, Mosquera, is quite common. I knew all odds were against me and I was also told not very many people watched channel eleven.

Shortly after I finished the interview, I thanked as many journalists and other employees as I could for wanting to help me and walked out the same doors I had come in through, happy to abandon the frosty studio and return to the thick humidity outside.

Forty-five minutes later I was back in the southern part of the city at the university, sitting across another white plastic table from my date. Her name was Claudia and I had met her a few days before by the university pool. As we talked, I confess I was not nervous. It was not for any misplaced sense of confidence with women, but it was due to the fact that I could not stop thinking about what had transpired during the morning. Claudia was interesting, funny, fiercely intelligent and gorgeous, but even her captivating dark eyes were no match for my daydreaming of what could happen as a result of the interview. We chatted over ice cream until the early afternoon, agreed to meet up again soon, and I hopped on a longer-than-usual bus trip back to the San Fernando area.

After knocking on the door back at the house around 5:00p.m., the girls were ecstatic when they saw me. They both hugged me and were beaming. This was not the typical response when I arrived, and I knew immediately something had happened.

"We have something to tell you, big news" one of them said. I looked at their eyes, studying their expression and trying to detect whether this was some sort of prank. Daniela asked Lucía if she wanted to tell me, then they decided they would both take turns telling me what had happened. Again, they did not know what I did that day, nor did they have a clue about the television interview. As we stood there in the entrance, it was Lucía who spoke first with a smile that grew wider with each word.

"A woman has been calling all afternoon saying that she is your aunt."

There was a short pause of silence and I stared at both of them again, unable to say a word. Their expressions were a mix of bewilderment and delight. It was as if they were both waiting for me to jump and shout, but I remained calm, more out of stern suspicion than anything else.

"I was home and the phone started ringing. I picked up and a lady was yelling and speaking really fast. I couldn't really understand and then I tried to tell her she had the wrong number." Daniela is generally quite calculated in her speech. She takes her time and is thoughtful with her words. However, she speeds up rapidly when the occasion demands it. This was the speediest I had ever heard her, which sent a signal to my instincts that this was not a joke at all. Her account of the day tells how confusing the day was for all of us:

I was sick when I woke up the morning. I received the phone call. I could not wait for the house to be empty so I could be sick and nurse my cold by myself. Eventually Lucía left for the university, Jake left to play soccer, and I moved to the couch to watch TV and nap. The sound of the telephone woke me up from a rather deep, medicine-induced sleep and I begrudgingly walked over to answer it. The woman on the other end of the line spoke so fast I could barely understand a word she was saying with my limited Spanish at the time. Something about a television station, eating lunch, some young man. Obviously, a wrong number.

"You have the wrong number," I eventually muttered, before hanging up the phone, though the thought lingered that the woman seemed frantic in the message she was trying to relay. I had sincerely hoped she found the right number and person she was looking for. After settling back onto the couch,

the phone rang again. It was the same woman repeating the same thing. "Señora, más despacio, por favor, slower please" I pleaded. It seemed the polite thing to do to allow her to speak before telling her once again that she had the wrong number. After I had my opportunity and as I was about to hang up, she said the name "Deisy Mosquera". What? At that point confusion really settled in. How was it possible that someone would be calling our house and using that name?

Having had numerous discussions with Jake about his adoption and looking over the adoption papers, discussing what things might be like if he were to find his biological mother, talking about the many what-ifs including the likely possibility that he might never connect with his family, this phone call seemed like such an impossibility.

At the time I had not known that Jake's day took a significant turn. I had wondered if someone from Chiquitines had somehow been in contact with Deisy Mosquera, but it seemed unlikely, and even more unlikely that they would have given out our home phone number. I asked the woman on the phone again to slow way down, and although she obliged, her sense of urgency and confusion remained. I managed to ascertain that her name was Ana, and she was a sister of Deisy Mosquera. Somehow, she had seen a young man on TV talking about her sister. Complete shock and disbelief set in and I could barely contain my excitement. I took down her number and immediately called Lucía at the university to explain the perplexing communication. She was equally stunned.

After a while Lucía called the house and explained that the woman had been home having lunch with her family with the TV on in the background--something they rarely turned on while eating. While not paying much mind to what was on, hearing her sister's name caught her attention and then she listened to the young man on TV. After calling the television station they gave her our home phone number and so began our poorly communicated conversation. Lucía dropped everything and came home, and together we sat around all afternoon trying to imagine all the ways this may have fallen into place, still not knowing why and how Jake made it to the TV station. The day seemed to take an eternity to pass by, as we were so excited to share the news. We also had no idea of where Jake was and had no way of communicating with him.

We listened intently for the gate to open at the bottom of the stairs so we could rush to the front door to greet him. When it finally did in the early evening, we ran to meet him and, in a flurry, explained the phone calls that occurred and with such enthusiasm and excitement, we declared that his family had been found!

My confusion from earlier in the day seemed to pale in comparison to that shown on Jake's face. He looked shocked, even a little scared, perhaps. I could not begin to understand what he must have been feeling and was surprised that he did not want to call Ana immediately and find answers, but in hindsight, it makes sense. Who wouldn't need time to process a lifetime of questions that you think may never be answered, all of a sudden being available with the push of a few buttons? So, we waited.

There are moments in life when one is left truly speechless. There are moments when, if one pays attention, time is suspended and all sounds, fears and hopes simply disappear. Such was that moment for me. I felt paralyzed with a mix of happiness and simultaneous disbelief. Still, as true as I wanted it to be and as much as I wanted to run through the streets out of sheer joy, I managed to suppress those feelings out of fear it was not true. I did not want to submit myself to pure bliss only to be woken up by the tiniest of details that could completely derail my euphoria. The girls advised me to take some time to process and decide if I wanted to go meet Ana that same night. I knew I did, but I sprinted down to the Parque del Perro first to try and call my parents to tell them the news. I could not reach anyone. That would have been approximately 2:30p.m. Pacific time in the U.S. so they were both still busy working. I jogged back up the street and hill to our house, then took the longest cold shower I could tolerate. After pacing back and forth in my room for a few moments just trying to think about how to *think* about the situation, I decided to call. I stepped out in the hallway, the tiles were cool under my bare feet, and I slowly pushed the numbers on the phone while looking at the piece of paper Daniela wrote Ana's number on.

"*Aló*?" answered the voice on the other end. Initially no words would come out but then I managed to mumble something resembling a quick introduction of who I was and asking if she was Ana. She erupted and, precisely as Daniela had described, she rattled off a series of incomprehensible phrases in an accent I was not familiar with. Once I was able to slow her down, I understood her asking if I would come to her house that evening. I knew I wanted to, but there was something I needed to know first. I needed to be certain this woman was who she was saying she was. Cali is the third largest city in the country. What guarantee did I have that this was not merely a desperate person trying to cash in on a skinny gringo and pose as his family to take advantage of him? Somehow, I remembered I did not mention my biological mother's birthday during the interview. Ana would have to know it if she was truly my aunt. So I asked.

"Cuándo es el cumpleaños de mi mamá biológica[10]*?"* I said, immediately proud of my pronunciation.

"My sister's? It's January twelfth." She did not have to think twice about it, nor consult any other people. There was no hesitation in her voice at all.

And, more importantly, her answer was correct.

Sweat instantly seized my palms, my heart rate jumped, and I felt a warm rush throughout my body. With that simple reply, Ana extinguished all doubt in my mind. That was it.

I found my biological mother's family.

---

10 When is my biological mother's birthday?

CHAPTER 4

Meeting Myself

MEETING ONE'S BIOLOGICAL FAMILY FOR THE FIRST time is a daunting endeavor – fraught with countless unknowns. There are people available to listen and offer advice, numerous blogs, books and other materials to learn what others have done in similar situations; but even so, there is no right or wrong course of action.

As I hung up the phone after the brief conversation with my long-lost aunt Ana, the bewilderment of the moment weighed heavily on my shoulders. My mind raced as I tried to fathom what it meant to find my family – how it would change my life, shape my future and significantly alter my self perception. I abruptly became the only person I knew with two families. There was no one in my vast social network, spanning a handful of countries, who I could lean on for advice or guidance about how the next weeks, months and years would unfold. I would need to rely wholly on myself.

We decided to go for it – to meet each other that very night. My attitude was there was nothing to lose and everything to gain. Carlos, the girls' resolute uncle who knew the city like the back of his hand, was summoned to drive us to Ana's house on the far eastern side of the city, in a neighborhood called Ciudad Córdoba. Curiously, I was warned by friends and people at Chiquitines to never go to that part of the city because, as in many other places, people fear what they do not know or understand.

Carlos instructed us to wait for him in the Parque del Perro to be picked up around 8:00p.m. Little by little, I prepared myself mentally to be stay present and enjoy each moment. I do not remember which shirt I chose nor what kind of pants I put on as I prepared for the evening. All I recall was grabbing my copy of the adoption documents Agatha gave me a couple years earlier to show as proof of my connection to the family. If I encountered questions or any skepticism from them, I could present the documents. Perhaps it was because of an impatient desire to confirm everything. Surely my new aunt Ana would want to piece together the story. I felt I owed her and the others waiting to meet me that luxury.

We walked down the street to the park without feeling rushed. It was then that I realized fear overcame me. I was terrified. I wanted to be perfect for my new family. Perhaps more than perfect; but how could I achieve such perfection without even speaking their language fluently? My frustration gave way to excitement as eventually we piled into the back of Carlos' jeep and began our voyage eastward.

The Distrito Aguablanca of Cali, the massive eastern district of the city in which Ciudad Córdoba exists, is home to a dizzying number of internally displaced families (Colombian families, mostly black, from other cities and towns forced to flee their homes because of the armed conflict), pervasive poverty and rampant gang activity. Any internet search for Distrito Aguablanca of Cali results in headlines detailing homicides and other forms of violence. It is an area that remains, to a large degree, virtually forgotten by the local government. These are the things I had heard from friends during those first few months of my trip, so I was apprehensive about charging into the neighborhood, especially at night. People filled my head with ideas about thieves waiting behind every corner and tight-knit communities where outsiders stood out, immediately drawing shady attention.

As we drove, the delusions in my head made me expect to see some expression of violence each time we came to a stop sign. Conversely, I saw nothing alarming at all; just people in the streets walking, eating, drinking beer, watching television and playing in billiard halls. And then I realized something: almost all of my friends and acquaintances there in Cali were white or mixed, none were black. In the Aguablanca, it is predominately black. It was a valuable lesson to understand many people back home in Tacoma as well in Cali were misguided by the same falsehoods and wrongful assumptions that predominately black neighborhoods were not to be trusted or frequented.

The further east we pushed, the more impoverished the neighborhoods appeared. A few dirt roads appeared, barely visible in the dim lights between a few streetlights and small parks. On one street, our senses were momentarily held captive by an immediate stench of garbage, then sewage. The next street blared with music as a street party began. We pushed on and Carlos appeared noticeably confused about the directions. He stopped and asked someone for help, regained his confidence, and we continued on our way. As it turned out, we were very close to our destination and only needed to continue straight down a narrow concrete street a short distance and turn left onto 48A street. We already arrived in the Ciudad Córdoba neighborhood. On the corner there was a two-story white building with what looked like blue trim. The street-level part had the word *panadería* above the white bars over windows and countertops. There were a few people standing around, sipping on sodas and eating various bread snacks. To our immediate right was a wide park with a few pruned short trees. The fence that lined it had a small brick and cement wall underneath that seemed to wrap around the entire park. Short bushes lined the sidewalk and followed us as we made our way to 48A street. Our jeep turned left, and we slowed down to look closely at the house numbers on either side of the narrow street.

Suddenly, someone yelled "*ahí está*, there it is!" and Carlos parked the jeep, turned off the ignition and we started to climb out. I glanced at the house to our left and caught a glimpse of someone in a chair or couch sitting close to the window. When the jeep was turned off, that person inside jumped to their feet and within seconds there were people coming out of the door immediately to the right of the window to greet us.

The first person I made eye contact with was the woman standing in the doorway with her arms folded. She had tears in her dark eyes, and she stood shaking her head slightly from side to side. I do not remember anything the others around me were doing, nor do I remember why or how I knew the woman before me was Ana, the same one who had seen me on television and who had made the phone call earlier that day.

My feet and legs felt heavy as I walked slowly toward her. I felt a rush of nerves then immediate calm as I imagined what I would say. No words came out. It was probably better that way. In the doorway, we locked each other in a hug that represented the single most triumphant moment of my life. The search for my biological family was officially over. Time, which is normally such a reliable companion, stood frozen. Ana embraced me with a fervor and warmth words fail to convey. She stood, motionless, as her tears fell from her eyes, streaking cheeks. The shock of the moment left me verbally paralyzed other than uttering the same phrase repeatedly, "*mucho gusto, tía*, nice to meet you, aunt." I was overjoyed and excited but also at a loss for words. My cheeks were wet with her tears and I just kept hugging. Somehow, we ended up back inside her home, all of us congregating in her small living room and occupying all the furniture and space available.

I shook hands with two young boys, a tall man in his forties, the large woman who I saw jump excitedly upon our arrival, and another woman who I learned could neither hear, nor speak. The two boys were Ana's sons, the younger named Milciades and the other named Leider. The older man was Ana's partner, also named Milciades; he was the first to see me on the television interview. The deaf-mute woman was his sister. And finally, the larger woman was Ninfa, my uncle Ciro's partner who had come from their house in the Decepaz neighborhood once she heard the news of my existence.

The mix of Cali and *paisa* accents from Carlos and Lucía was a stark contrast to the Tumaco/Cali accent used by my new family members. The accents seemed to spar with each other in midair. I perceived there was a bit of an awkward pause as we settled in to ask and answer questions due to the linguistic differences. Lucía quickly became my interpreter. I answered questions about my family in the United States. Ana was particularly interested in my upbringing. She wanted to know if I had been well-fed, taken care of, given a proper education and provided consistent health care. The older Milciades, while cordial and inviting, seemed distant during our conversation and our interactions were few. Milciades Jr. however, pressed me for random vocabulary words in English and his brother joined in. Ninfa sat, silently watching and grinning from ear to ear; I remember her saying something about my uncle Ciro being very excited to meet me.

I passed the copy of the adoption documents to Ana and watched as she read, more tears followed. She paused, looked up at me, back at the documents and let out a long sigh as she tried to wipe her eyes with her hands. She grabbed my hand and squeezed tightly, gasping for air between sobs. "*Es que no entiendo por qué mi hermana nunca dijo nada. No sabíamos nada. Tu mamá nunca nos dijo nada.*" I turned to Lucía, anxious to know what Ana said. She stated slowly, "she's saying she doesn't understand why your mother never said anything. She says your mother never told them anything." It was then that I realized my very existence was a surprise to them. My biological mother made the decision to conceal her pregnancy as well as my birth from her entire family. It made sense why Ana was so hysterical on the phone. Seeing my television interview must have been such a nerve-wracking moment of disbelief for her. The family members she called when she learned about the news likely felt just as dumbfounded. Ana had yet to contact the rest of my new extended family in the small coastal city of

Tumaco, tucked away in Colombia's most southwestern corner. My brother was one of those people.

We gathered around the phone and dialed his cell number. I really had no clue what to say. What does one say over the phone to his brother he has never met in person? With my limited vocabulary and sense of overall shock in the moment, I managed to ask a simple question: "who is María Deisy Mosquera for you?" He paused slightly and finally offered, "*ella es mi mamá, por qué*? She's my mom, why?" I responded and said that the same was true for me and he laughed, saying he did not have any brothers. He was convinced he was an only child and, after some back and forth, demanded to speak with Ana. I passed the phone and needed no translation to see that Ana had to do considerable work to convince him of the situation. Eventually, we decided he would come to Cali to visit me in December and we said our goodbyes.

It was time to ask them about my biological mother. When I did, the room fell silent. Their reaction suggested she had passed away but then, the older Milciades made a circular motion with his hand next to his ear and said flatly, "*ella está jodida*." I gathered from his gesture that he meant she was crazy. I waited for more explanation since this obviously meant she was still alive. Ana turned to me and said slowly so I could understand her, that Deisy, as they called her, disappeared. Again. Lucía took over and what I came to understand was that Deisy would appear for short intervals of time, sometimes weeks, sometimes months and then vanish for extended periods without a trace. During these times away she would not communicate with the rest of the family. She was, as they all put it, "lost and crazy." She preferred to spend time with families she would work as a domestic worker for. She despised the family, and to make matters more complicated, she was deaf, so communication when she did choose to appear was incomplete at best. I do not know what I expected or hoped to learn about her, but what they told me took me by complete surprise. At once I pitied her and wanted to do all in my power to fix her problems. My mind jumped to a fantasy with me taking her to a doctor's appointment to see what could be done with her hearing situation. We both were smiling widely in my quick daydream. I promised myself that night I would help if I ever got the chance to meet her. Not only did it seem like the right thing to do, it was also exactly what I wanted to do.

By that time, it was getting late and Carlos needed to get home. We exchanged more specific information about where the girls and I were living, gave hugs and handshakes and we were out the door. Ninfa needed a ride back home to Decepaz; she and Carlos spoke the entire way to her house. I sat with my eyes glues to the window, wide awake but unable to speak because I was trying to process everything.

Decepaz more closely resembled how I imagined the Distrito Aguablanca to be. Houses were all structures of brick and cement, there was little lighting, hardly any trees, it was dusty and very obviously one of the most impoverished neighborhoods in the city. Music blared and I noticed a few half naked children scurrying around clapping and skipping with their flip flops in the glow of the streetlamps. The jeep came to a halt next to a small parking lot and we got out, crossed the street and made our way into an alleyway. A single wooden ladder stretched up to the second floor of a concrete balcony with no railing, a darkly painted steel door and brick/cement walls. Ninfa climbed up the ladder effortlessly and motioned for us to join her. I climbed up and was shocked at their living conditions; sheets were fashioned into doors that failed to keep out swarms of hungry mosquitos. I received a few bites within seconds of sitting down. A small picture hung on a plastic pipe which extended from the brick and cement wall and there were a couple of small lamps which provided dim light. A gray television with a blurry image of a female speaker created ambient noise in the small room. Suddenly Ninfa placed a giant plastic bottle of soda and a large strawberry cake on a small wooden table that we sat around. I met her four children, four more cousins; Briggith (twelve), Cristian (fourteen), Ingrid Vanessa (fifteen) and Alejandra (eighteen). Alejandra was the most talkative while the others smiled widely but hardly spoke. I learned Briggith was pronounced "bree-jeet" and that everyone affectionately called Ingrid "Pili." Ninfa insisted we call my uncle Ciro on the phone. He was working in Bogotá. Once we had him on the line, I struggled to understand him. He has a very thick Tumaco accent and also speaks extremely fast. He is a jubilant man and promised to come to Cali as soon as possible so we could meet and mentioned that if I happened to be in Bogotá, then we could meet while there as well. We all sat and talked while eating the cake for some time, mostly answering questions about life in the U.S. and my adoptive family. When it was time to leave, I invited them over for dinner at our house in San Fernando the following Friday. It seemed appropriate to throw a party for such an occasion. Moments later, we were off in the jeep again to Carlos' house in the Villanueva neighborhood, then caught a cab which took us the rest of the way home.

It was late when we opened the door back at our house. The rawness of the day left me emotionally drained and I could not sleep. I wanted to call everyone I knew back in the U.S., but I was unable to because the international call stores were all closed at that hour. I laid awake, making a game out of trying to imagine all I would discover about the family in the weeks and months to follow. What were their interests and preferences? What hopes and aspirations did they have? What did we have in common? Which topics would we eventually clash over? How did they feel about me? How and when would I finally earn their trust—and they earn mine?

I awoke in my bed, after only a handful of hours of rest, to the sound of a neighbor playing vallenato music. The scent of freshly brewed coffee was in the air along with the tedious thickness of the familiar humidity. It felt like any other morning, yet everything had changed.

Exactly where in the house or what time I found myself weeping hysterically on the phone with my parents is not important. I lost it, almost choking from my own tears, as I heard myself thanking them for all they did for my sister and I, for all the sacrifices they made on my behalf, for the countless hours helping me with homework, for instilling a sense of pride and dignity in me, for gently insisting my sister and I have goals, for expecting good things from us and helping us to achieve our aspirations, for the undeniable and unwavering support they provided in all aspects of our young lives and for providing us with a nurturing home. For their eternal and truly unconditional admiration and love. While meeting my biological family, I did not shed any tears. I was too engulfed by the immensity of what transpired; but during that phone call, when I heard my mom's voice as she said, "we're truly happy for you", I knew she was sincere. I knew that *she* knew what a monumental moment it was for me.

I knew, even if she could not completely understand what I was feeling, she deeply wanted to. I have witnessed nothing so pure in all of my days.

I wept out of a sense of relief. At twenty years old, I was still quite materialistic. Seeing the way most Colombians I saw lived began to transform me into a humbler and more thoughtful version of myself. I felt relieved to know I had not grown up in the crippling poverty I saw around me. I felt lucky. And ultimately, I cried out of guilt as well. Adoption provided me with opportunities I simply would not have had if I would have been raised in Colombia. It was a similar feeling from when I visited the orphanage for the first time. I did not feel saved, but I did feel fortunate.

My grandma Marge, Isabella, Me, my mom Cindy in Cali – 1984

REPUBLICA DE COLOMBIA

PORTE / Passport
AB 343657

APELLIDOS / Surnames
MOSQUERA

NOMBRE / Given Names
ALFONSO

FECHA DE NACIMIENTO / Date of birth
Abril 03 1984

SEXO / Sex
Masculino

LUGAR DE NACIMIENTO / Place of birth
Cali-Valle

DOCUMENTO DE IDENTIDAD / Identity card
———

ESTADO CIVIL/Marital st
Soltero

TALLA / Height
———

OJOS / Color of eyes
———

NARIZ / Nose
———

FECHA DE EXPEDICION / Date of issue
Noviembre 08 1984

CIUDAD / City
Cali-Valle

FECHA DE VENCIMIENTO / Date of expiry
Noviembre 08 1989

DEL TITULAR / Holder's signature

AUTORIDAD / Authority
JEFE SECCION DE PASAPORTES

My first passport – 1984

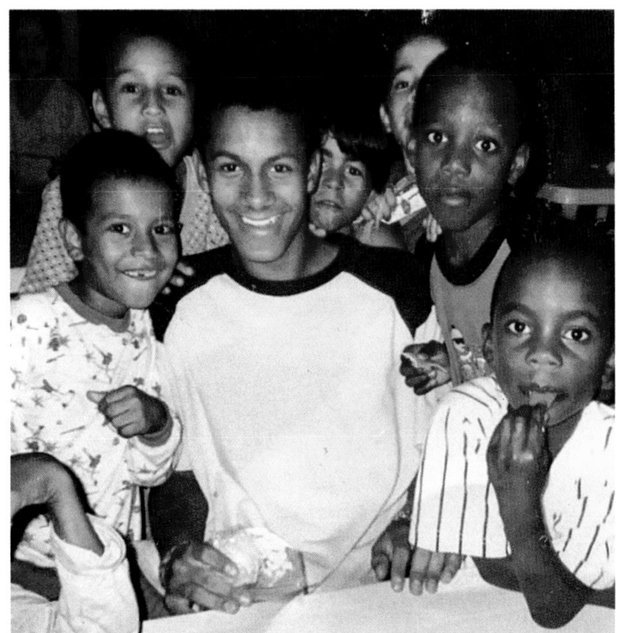

First visit to Chiquitines Adoption Center in Cali – 2002

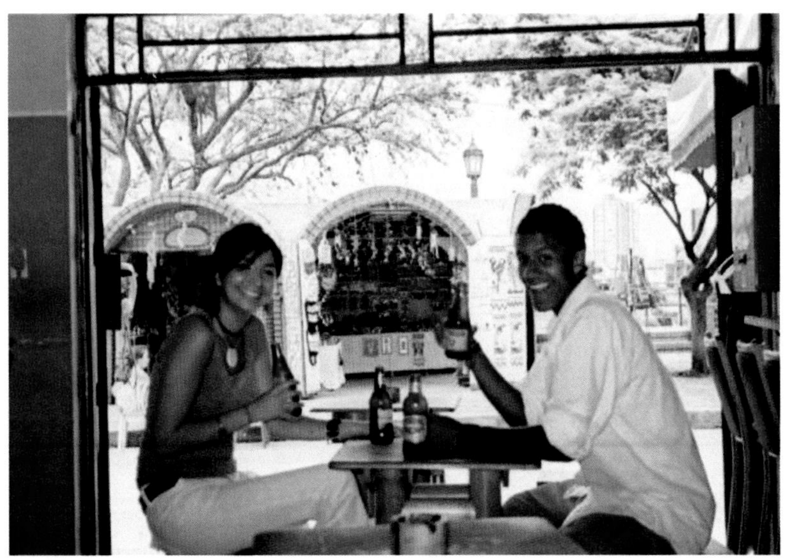

Daniela and me in Cali – 2004

Cousin Cristian, Briggith, mom, me, aunt Ninfa, Alejandra, Pili – 2004

Heartfelt hug between aunt Ninfa and mom in Cali – 2004

A drink with aunt Nubia and Jhon Jairo during first visit to Tumaco – 2005

El Morro beach in Tumaco – 2005

Para Jake Tritón

Jake, desde el día 26 de octubre del 2004 que supimos de su existencia, nos sentimos muy contentos, con una alegría que no sabemos como describir. solo sabemos que sin saber que existía un miembro más en nuestra familia y que es un ser maravilloso.

Jake, gracias por llegar a nosotros. que apesar de ser una familia. humilde tenemos el gusto de ser una familia unida, y que lo acogemos con todo nuestro corazón y le damos gracias a Dios. por que llegó a darnos una de las alegrías más grandes que hemos tenido.

gracias por permitirnos. disfrutar de su presencia y de unos ratos maravillosos. de la misma forma. damos muchas gracias a tu familia. por averte acogido dandote tanto amor. cariño comprensión y sobre todo por haber hecho de ti una persona. tan. humana bondadosa y tan de buenos sentimientos. gracias por ser como eres y por aver llegado a nosotros. y esperamos volver a verte muy pronto y seguir al tanto de tu vida nos gustaría saber de ti de lo que hagas de ahora en adelante.

Mucha suerte, que Dios te bendiga siempre
tu familia que te quiere mucho

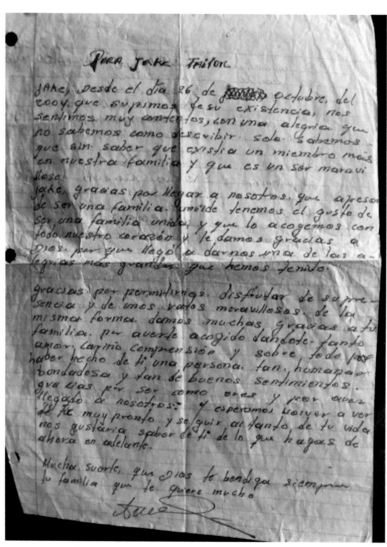

The letter from family members in Tumaco – 2005

A few days after meeting Deisy in Cali – 2005

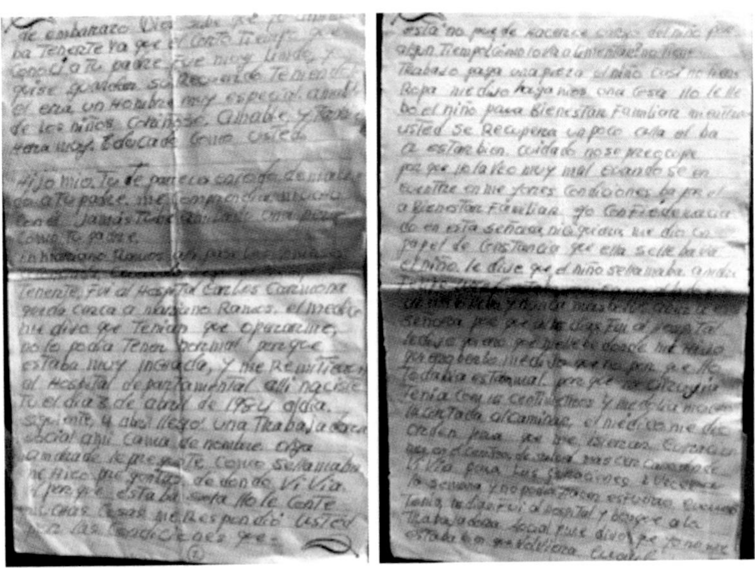

Two pages from the letter from Deisy in Cali – 2005

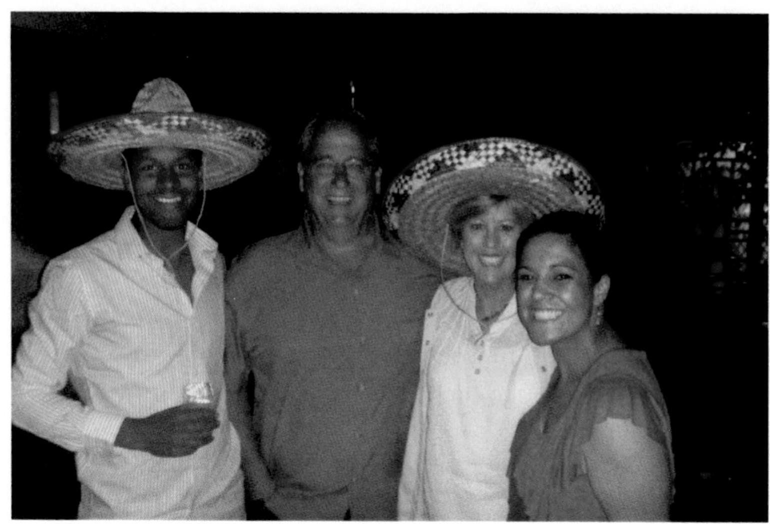

Me, dad, mom and my sister Diana – 2011

Juan Antonio, Isabella, me and Laura in Cali – 2016

With the attendees at the Alamor event in Cali – 2017

Christmas Eve in Cali with some of the biological family – 2018

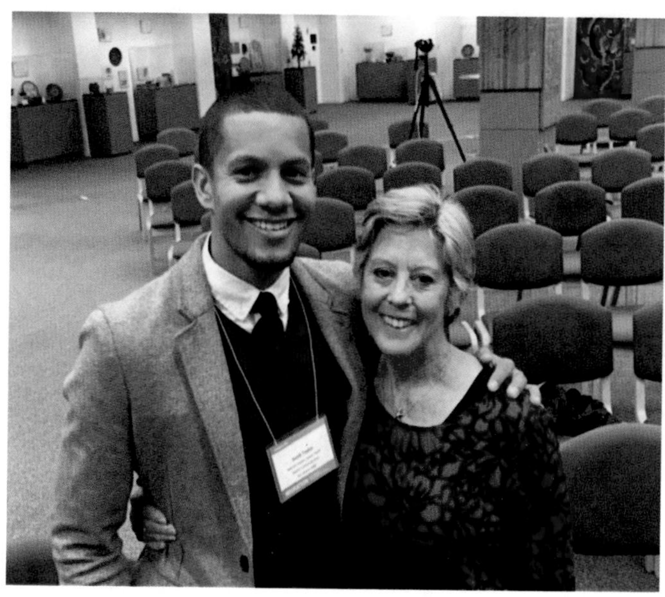

Me and mom at an event in Tacoma, WA – 2018

Colombian adoptees Diego, Astrid, me and Astrid's daughter, Maya in Seattle – 2019

With Milciades and aunt Ana in Cali – 2019

CHAPTER 5
Chasing Deisy

THE DAYS THAT FOLLOWED WERE SUCH A BLUR. Messages from home poured in with words of congratulations and, in at least a few instances, caution. I was advised against lending money or trusting my new family too quickly. In my haste to comprehend everything that was happening, I felt annoyed because all the advice coming my way was from people who really had no idea what I was experiencing. Their concern was genuine, and I appreciated their words. However, they could not truly empathize. I ignored the advice, dismissing it as unfounded and unwanted. In those few days, I went to Chiquitines to tell them I would be taking an extended break from my English teaching duties to focus on my newly found family.

The Chiquitines staff understood and assured me I would always be welcome to spend time with the children and staff there. My second stop that day brought me back to Telepacífico, where my television interview was filmed. I brought freshly cut sunflowers from the market to show my appreciation for their having helped me find my family. The flowers were received with extended hugs, smiles and high-fives. The journalists who helped me with the interview insisted I keep them updated on how the next weeks and months developed. During those first three or four days after meeting my family, I alternated between visiting the three points of the west-east triangle of the city that consisted of San Fernando, Ciudad Córdoba and Decepaz. One of my top priorities was to learn the bus routes even better between all the parts of the city I would be frequenting with fresh determination.

On Monday, November first, I was in Decepaz and had just eaten a warm plate of rice, beans, fried plantains and chicken with my cousins and Ninfa. Getting up to take my plate to the kitchen, something on the small wooden table caught my eye. I quietly examined it while I stood with my plate in my hands. It was a familiar signature, the same I saw in my adoption documents – it belonged to Deisy.

> *Lunes 1 de Noviembre*
>
> *When I saw the same handwriting as on that one piece of paper in Chiquitines on the table at Ninfa's, I almost fell over. That, for me, was the defining moment that proves all of this is not some spectacular dream.*

My picture of Deisy was becoming more and more clear as a result of what people offered, oftentimes at random. We would be talking about things unrelated to family and all of a sudden, someone would start telling a story about how Deisy tricked them, how she stole from them or how she fought with them over something miniscule. It was not until I was at my cousin Jhoana's house in the Manuela Beltrán neighborhood, helping her with English homework, that I caught a glimpse of this mysterious woman's personality.

Lunes 15 de Noviembre

After some ten minutes of English lessons, Jhoana's grandmother and someone else came into the room and we chatted about the differences between the U.S. and Colombia. Then I asked Jhoana what Deisy is like, because I had heard very little about her personality. She told me she loved to cook, knit clothing and that was quite reserved but had more trust in Jhoana than anyone else in the family.

Hearing about Deisy's personality was a pleasant shift from listening about her numerous mistakes and affinity for burning bridges within the family. It made her more human to me, more likeable and my desire to meet her face-to-face grew fierce. Only a few days later, again in Decepaz, it seemed I would have my opportunity.

> *Jueves 18 de Noviembre*
>
> *We ate lentils with rice and aguapanela. I slept for about two hours and Ninfa arrived at 8:30p.m. I spoke with her and Ana about today being Leider's birthday. The telephone rang and I looked with anticipation as Ninfa grew animated. A woman named Teresa had called, who is Willy's daughter (one of Ciro's cousins whom I do not know). They said Deisy had appeared. I did not know what to say or think. So, all is set: tomorrow I will go with my cousin Alejandra at 6:30a.m. to a hospital in the Mojica neighborhood because Deisy has an appointment there. It is too bad I do not have the copies of the adoption papers to show her.*

The phone call from Teresa meant word was spreading fast amongst all extended family members, friends and neighbors alike, in a search effort spanning who knows how many neighborhoods throughout the city to connect me with my biological mother. It was overwhelming and exhilarating at the same time.

The next day, we woke up early, had a quick snack and were out the door just as planned. It felt as though Alejandra was just as determined as I. We hailed the first taxi we saw and sped off further south through the brick and cement maze of Aguablanca. The sun was already burning through the taxi's windows. Once at the hospital, we noticed a line of approximately thirty people waiting to get through the main doors to seek treatment. The two doors were painted white and had large rectangular windows in them. Additional windows around the entrance made it easy to see it was packed inside. My feet ached as we stood eyeing the line of people; they were infected due to excessive mosquito bites. I walked inside and found a spot on a hard chair with a view of the line outside. Alejandra remained outside and said she would come get me as soon as she found Deisy. Ten minutes passed while I sat observing the busy waiting room. Nurses, doctors and other medical personnel hurried around frantically. People shouted rampantly and the few who were on cell phones had to practically scream to be heard. There was a single fan in the waiting room but outside I could see the heat hovering above the dirt. The fan was powerless in its attempts to calm the humidity. Many people sat fanning their faces with newspapers or with flip flops they took off their feet.

I glanced through the window and noticed Alejandra bolting towards the entrance. She entered with such force that almost everyone looked up at her and she called to me, "*vení, ya llegó, ya llegó*! Come, she arrived, she arrived!" I got up as quickly as I could and together, we jogged out the door toward the back of the line, my heart beating much faster than my feet were carrying me. Once at the back of the line Alejandra stopped, she looked back toward the hospital entrance, then again to the back of the line. Her eyes darted back and forth, then to the street, then once more to the hospital entrance. She turned, said nothing, and started walking back toward the hospital while asking people in line questions. She appeared to be asking if anyone had seen Deisy and was describing her as the short lady with glasses who walked strangely. I stood, paralyzed with confusion. Alejandra walked back to me shaking her head and looking at the ground, clearly disappointed.

> *Sábado 20 de Noviembre*
>
> *I was meters away from meeting my biological mother but when we got out there, she already left. It turns out Alejandra had made eye contact with her and she asked "qué pasó? What happened?" Alejandra motioned for her to wait, she must have suspected something, then she was gone.*

This incident forced me to ponder why Deisy was so elusive with the family. What exactly transpired between all of them to inspire this kind of mistrust? The reality was she skipped a medical appointment because her niece asked her to wait for something. In her mind, the only decision available was to leave immediately. Why?

Dejected, we rode back to Decepaz to tell everyone what happened. Ninfa shrugged in silence, shaking her head slightly while she washed dishes in the sink. My cousins mumbled that

Deisy's actions did not surprise them. Their collective unsurprised reaction was a clear indication to me they were accustomed to such behavior from her.

As I sat on the couch, I paid no attention to the conversation going on around me. Although I had not met her yet, my mind played images of Deisy wherever she was in the city at that time. Was she stewing over why her niece was so frantic outside the hospital? What did she suspect, if anything? Obviously, she could not have imagined her son she never told anyone about was sitting on the other side of the doors she waited to walk through for her appointment. Surely, she wondered how Alejandra knew she would be there at that time. My daydreaming was cut short by the music being turned up and the day melted into a blend of lounging, listening to music, impromptu English lessons, more plates of rice and, ultimately, me getting on a bus and going home.

* * *

Anticipation was building around our house for the arrival of Carolina, a twenty-year-old model from Spain. Daniela and Lucía had asked me weeks earlier if I would be okay with her staying with us for couple weeks. Apparently, she was a friend of a friend of Lucía's. I was quick to answer an enthusiastic "yes" and was abruptly shot down by Lucía. "Don't get too excited. She's way out of your league."

The day Carolina was supposed to arrive in Cali was Thursday November twenty-fifth which happened to be Thanksgiving that year back in the States. Daniela took the lead as the official Thanksgiving coordinator and we had a few friends over for some food that included a random chunk of turkey. Nobody knew where this mysterious chunk of turkey had come from and I recall it tasting like anything but turkey. Shortly after our meal, it was time to go to the airport. Carlos came to pick us up, and we were off.

Once at the airport, raindrops bounced off our windows and the pavement in front of the international arrivals exit grew damp within a few minutes. The insides of the windows fogged with our breath and I kept wiping it with my sleeve to catch a glimpse of Carolina, who I was told, would have a bright red and yellow suitcase. As my head moved from left to right looking at people coming out to greet loved ones, I noticed three blonde women standing together. Two of the women were tall, one more heavy-set than the other, and the third was petite, bent over her backpack searching for something. I commented to Daniela about how good it was to see more tourists coming to the country since it meant Colombia's international image was improving. She agreed and the jeep suddenly became too quiet for comfort. I looked at everyone and they were looking right at me in anticipation of a reaction on my behalf. I awkwardly laughed and turned to keep searching for Carolina. The three blonde women were still there, and the third was looking at her watch. For some strange reason she seemed familiar. I wiped the window again to get a better look. The women were talking, and the petite woman smiled. I realized it was a smile I had seen many times; in fact, I grew up seeing that smile. My mom came to surprise me on Thanksgiving in Colombia, and she traveled with a former neighbor and her daughter. I whipped my head back towards everyone and the jeep erupted in laughter. I opened the door and limped quickly to greet them. "What are you doing here?" I shouted at her as we locked each other in a hug. "Surprise" she said. Of course, once back in the jeep I asked about Carolina. "Haha, you dumbass. She doesn't exist! The whole thing was a trick." Daniela and Lucía high-fived each other as we made our way back into the city.

My mom, her friend and her friend's daughter had reservations at the Hotel Residencia Stein, which is now called the Hotel Stein Colonial, in northern Cali. It was an appropriate choice since it was the same hotel my mom and grandma had stayed 20 years earlier when they came to finalize my adoption and take me back to the States. The hotel, nestled amongst large trees and surrounded by an intricate stone wall, used to be home to the Swiss consulate. Throughout the 1980s, 1990s and to a lesser degree today, adopting families would stay there while finalizing adoptions. It was and remains a good way for adopting families to network and is particularly convenient for European couples coming from the same countries or, in some cases, the same city. My mom mentioned it was an obvious choice for them for this reason and confessed they had planned the surprise for at least a month. She even knew about the fictitious Carolina.

Her visit represented the perfect opportunity to fulfill one of my most coveted dreams: to have my mom meet my biological family, or at least a handful of them. My growing confidence with Spanish meant I would be able to establish myself as the linguistic bridge between her and my new family members. We wasted no time inviting Carlos's family, Ninfa and her kids, and a few of our friends over for dinner and dancing.

A few days later my mom, my aunt Ana and I met and walked to the main hospital on 5th street - the hospital where I was born. My determination to locate Deisy had not weakened and Ana suggested looking for clues at the hospital which, according to her, was the only place Deisy visited with any regularity. Rumor had it she was constantly in and out of medical appointments, visits to clinics and pharmacies to fill prescriptions. The Hospital Departamental Universitario del Valle is arguably the most important hospital in the entire southern half of the country. As such, it is generally very busy. It if had been just my mom and me going into the chaos of those hallways, I doubt we would have been successful in our mission; from my perspective, Colombian hospitals were not similar to those in North America. The glaring difference I saw was how chaotic everything seemed. Ana marched with us, firing questions to anyone who walked by in rapid Spanish. Her voice was lost in the buzz of the hospital corridor. I watched as she eventually disappeared in the crowd, leaving my mom and I to wonder what to do with ourselves.

She returned moments later and spoke slowly to inform us she found a file with some of Deisy's records. As a direct family member, she had access to said file and so did I. My original idea was to read the file and search for addresses or phone numbers and then track her down with that information. Upon reading the first couple of pages and translating for my mom, I started to realize the extent of Deisy's suffering.

Lunes 29 de Noviembre

Most of the file was about her jaw and the work she's had on it. The last time she was there in the hospital was February 24th of this year for being hit by a car which broke her leg. There was an X-ray of her jaw and more things on that.

There, in that hectic mixture of humidity, crying babies and hurried nurses, I tried to imagine what it would feel like to be hit by a car. I wondered who was there to help her when it happened if anyone. It was obvious she would not have called the family for help in those times. Who did she contact? Did anyone visit her hospital bed as she recovered or did she suffer alone in silence? My aunt shrugged and flatly said she did not know of any of the things we were reading about. "*Tu mamá prefiere estar muy alejada de la familia*[11]."

The three of us walked back outside to the busy street and hailed a taxi to take us to Ciudad Córdoba so mom could see Ana's house. Once we got to the house, we spent the afternoon talking about different family members and life in general. As one might imagine, they had plenty of questions for each other, although it was clear that my mom was a bit uneasy. I also felt considerable tension in the air while the three of us sat together. The two women, although relatively close in age, come from polar opposite backgrounds. In that moment on the couch, I was the interpreter sitting between them, but I also felt as if my arms were the opposite ends of a large rope in a tug of war. They were not doing anything overtly aggressive, but it was obvious to me they were subtly vying for my affection. I asked my mom to recount the afternoon:

I remember very clearly the message that Ana was sending. When we got out of the taxi and were walking down the sidewalk, she clung to your arm in a very possessive manner. Often, there was not room on the sidewalk for the three of us to walk side by side, but she never let go of your arm. I was then the one to walk behind the two of you. Her message of blood

11 Your mom prefers to be very far from the family.

being thicker than water was very, very clear to me. Of anyone in your family, she was the one that I did not trust. I felt like she was a threat to me in the sense that I was not your true or real family. I do not feel that way anymore, but it took quite a long time for me to feel okay about her and not feel uncomfortable about what her intentions were with you.

I wonder if my mom was justified in thinking these things and if my aunt was truly attempting to send a message, as my mom suggested. Perhaps the tension I perceived was simply my mom's uneasiness. It took time for me to realize that, while I desired for my adoptive and biological families to meet for decades, it was simultaneously the culmination of what my parents originally feared: having the biological family want me back; thus, unleashing an eternal unspoken battle of allegiances. I think about what might have been rushing through Ana's mind in those moments as well. The family had no idea I existed before news spread of the television interview with Telepacífico. Numerous people in the family, as well as friends, declared the events as nothing short of a miracle. Also, worth keeping in mind, is how many people in Colombia perceive life in the United States; the popular misconception being that we're all millionaires. In essence, Ana and others may have hoped I represented the financial salvation of the family. Given all of this, her behavior seems natural to me.

My mom and her friends departed Colombia almost as quickly as they arrived. Together, we saw different parts of Cali and she was able to meet a small part of my biological family, albeit with certain reservations. I wished she could have stayed for much longer, perhaps even a month more to really get a feel for the culture.

There was so much more I desperately wanted to show her – so many more experiences I sought to share with her. If it would have been completely up to me, we would have spent every day with different groups of my biological family. Deep down, I needed her to grapple with the same questions of race and privilege I was wrestling with, albeit from the vantage point of her own lived experiences as a white, North American woman. I wanted my mom to achieve a level of curiosity and, ultimately, understanding of the place I come from that reached far deeper than the superficial general expressions of Colombian culture. I wished the conversations with my biological family lasted longer, wished the questions and answers were more probing, maybe even more controversial in order for everyone to get a truly authentic glimpse into each other's personalities. However, my wishes proved to be unrealistic for the moment and to no fault of my mom's or of the biological family members she met. Still, I know our bond was strengthened significantly as a result of her visit. It speaks to her courage and truly unconditional love and support of me for her to confront her fear of potentially losing me to Colombia.

I am forever proud of her for taking that leap.

CHAPTER 6

Ñaño

BEFORE LONG, ANOTHER FAMILY MEMBER OF MINE was on his way to Cali to meet me. I was summoned to Ana's house after receiving a phone call saying my brother Jhon Jairo made the trip up from Tumaco to meet me. I stood in her bedroom chatting about Colombian politics with her while she rearranged clothes and candles on her dresser and small desk against her wall. Suddenly, we heard the doorbell ring and Jhon Jairo's voice rang out from downstairs. "*Y dónde e'tá mi hermano*[12]*?*" Ana yelped with excitement. I could not tell which of us was more thrilled.

My cousins, probably entranced by another telenovela, told him we were upstairs, and we heard quick heavy steps coming toward us. I desperately wanted to make a good impression on my brother and hoped we would establish a strong connection like those I was building with other members of the extended family. He burst into the room wearing Nike sneakers, red

12 And where's my brother?

athletic pants along with a red and blue NBA jersey. He immediately reminded me of a darker, more fit version of myself. There was silence as we stood for those first seconds examining each other, unsure of which words were the most appropriate. "*Abraza tu hermano!* Hug your brother!" Ana squealed while shoving Jhon Jairo toward me, her smile wide and her eyes beginning to tear.

Those first few moments were awkward because I could not understand much of what they said to each other. Jhon Jairo's accent was like listening to a machine gun, if a machine gun could speak Tumaco Spanish. I made progress in understanding the family's accent, but Jhon Jairo's was fresh from the coast, lively to the point of confusion. We did not cry; perhaps protecting our perceived masculinity was to blame, but we did walk back downstairs together, asking each other questions about our trips to Cali.

Downstairs we sat around the table to have some dinner Ana prepared. The items on the table were inevitable: rice, beans, salad and chicken soup. So many things raced through my head. What was being in the military like? Had my brother killed anyone? What was growing up in Tumaco like? Did he secretly despise me for being adopted? But, how could he? Still, did he? Would I ever know? Would I ever want to know?

The rice was hot and sticky, a perfect pairing with the heat in the house. The cool and frothy passion fruit juice was a welcome treat. I began to mix my food together on the plate, as I had always done. To my surprise, I was not the only one at the table who practiced this habit, deemed strange by so many back home. "*Qué estás haciendo, hombre*? What are you doing, man?" I looked up to see my brother smiling, mixing his food at the same time as me. The table laughed in unison. We were beginning to see we had a few things in common. We were both soccer fans, Colombia first, then Brazil, although my secondary loyalties have shifted since then. We both enjoyed walking, both fiercely defended our families and neither of us grew up with our biological mother. Jhon Jairo explained to me, slowly so I could understand as Ana and the boys listened and nodded, that Deisy sent him to live with aunts, uncles, cousins and our grandmother in Tumaco at a very young age. Along with everyone else, he had no idea she gave birth to another child. His words and tone tiptoed around resentment at the fact Deisy never sent him clothes, food, pictures, letters or money - nothing. As we finished dinner, he asked if I wanted to go for a walk. His request puzzled me because I felt anything he wanted or needed to say could be said in front of Ana and the boys, but I accepted.

We made our way outside to the long park a block away from Ana's house and found a small concrete bench to sit on with dark green paint on the back. The sun dipped behind the jagged mountains in the distance as a small-sided soccer game ensued in the dirt and grass before us. We each had a Quatro soda bottle in our hand, and as we sipped, Jhon Jairo began after a slight pause, "*quiero saber por qué fuiste adoptado y yo no. No estoy celoso, nada que ver, porque tengo mi familia aquí, pero ¿qué fue lo que pasó*[13]*?*"

I swallowed hard. It was a question that begged for and deserved a few hours of deep conversation to properly answer; but my Spanish was still limited. Even if I had the linguistic skills to express how I felt, and could effectively answer the question,

13 I want to know why you were adopted and I wasn't. I'm not jealous, not at all, because I have my family here. But what exactly happened?

I probably would have still responded with the very short and simply reply: *no sé*. He could clearly see I wanted to unload everything dashing through my mind, but he also understood I was struggling to answer, so he opted for 'yes' or 'no' questions instead. Did I like growing up in the States? Yes, and it had its struggles. Did my family treat me well? Yes! Did I have any children or a girlfriend? No. Why not! I was taking a break from dating. Did I ever want to live in Colombia? We will see. Did I have to do military service in the U.S.? No. Did I support the bilateral U.S. aid package called Plan Colombia? Not completely. Did I play any other sports than soccer? No. We went on and on interviewing each other with these types of questions for some time.

I was captivated but also revolted at how he described his time in the Colombian military. There was still evident anger in his voice as he divulged details of some of his missions, one including a helicopter ride in which he and fellow soldiers were dispatched near a river to search for fallen comrades' severed limbs, ears, fingers and other body parts after a confrontation with the Revolutionary Armed Forces of Colombia (or FARC). He expressed irritation at the fact that, as he put it, "los colombianos seguimos y seguramente seguiremos encerrados en una guerra civil porque gringos ricos quieren consumir cocaína para escaparse de sus vidas perfectas[14]." The wannabe journalist in me at the time wished I had a recorder. He paused and suggested we change the subject. I nodded. He continued to talk about his son, Dubin and then, he looked at me in the eye and said his partner, Gisela, was pregnant with their second. I shook his hand

14 Colombians continue to be locked in a civil war because rich gringos want to consume cocaine to escape from their perfect lives.

and congratulated him. "*Y qué piensas si le doy tu nombre*[15]*?*" He asked with a wide smile, although it felt more like a declaration. I felt honored and immediately approved. The boy would be named Jake Sebastián, although this would prove to be a challenge since the Colombian pronunciation would turn it to something more like "Jay" because the K is virtually non-existent in Spanish. I was ecstatic at the prospect of having someone named after me.

My new nephew would surely be the only Jake on the coast, perhaps even the country. The conversation shifted to jobs and I learned he was a mechanic and a taxi driver back in Tumaco. The military constantly asked him to come back, but he declined. They needed him; Colombia needed him; they would say. In a good week with his taxi (which he rented from someone else) he was making around 100,000 pesos which, back in 2004, was the equivalent to approximately $50.00 USD. In the military, he would be guaranteed a much more handsome income along with the countless benefits that accompany a military career in Colombia. However, he maintained that he preferred to be with his family and not in the jungle shooting and being shot at. It was getting late, and we decided to return to the house, still discussing the military and family. Similarly intriguing was something he mentioned before discussing the military, which I did not want to pry at in that moment. It seemed like a good topic for the next time we would see each other, in Tumaco.

> *Lunes 20 de Diciembre*
>
> *We talked about our mother and how he has not seen her in about ten years. But he is already accustomed*

15 And what do you think if I give him your name?

> *to not talking with her. He was raised by the aunts, uncles and Lucila in Tumaco. He lived with Deisy for a short time then went to Tumaco when he was nine. He never really got into studying even though the aunts and Lucila insisted. He prefers to walk long distances rather than take buses or taxis. He describes Tumaco with such pride. He paints it so well, like a hidden paradise to the south. He says everyone is friends, equals, and that you can go to any house and ask for some water and the people will give it to you. He told me about El Morro, the big bridge and the beaches on Sundays. We talked about differences between the people here in Cali and there, about work and about his time in the military. Scary stuff. He has been face-to-face with the guerrilla and the paramilitaries. He has had to pick up fallen compatriots and travel all over shooting and getting shot at. Before all that, he had to get involved in 'working' (as he put it) with coca leaves to get money. But he is done now. He worked in Putumayo and the Llanos with that. Now he wants to start up something like a clothing store...the idea is to concentrate on his family and children. One can tell he really cares about his son and the one that's on the way just by the way he talks about giving them education. In the picture he gave me, his son Dubin is wearing better shoes than he is.*

Before meeting Jhon Jairo, I had only been truly in awe of someone on one other occasion and it was when I met my childhood hero, Hall of Famer, Ken Griffey Jr. who played baseball for the Seattle Mariners. My brother, in that time sitting on the bench in the park, surpassed Griffey instantly. One could rightly say I saw my brother as a sort of hero, having survived arduous, unsafe conditions in the jungle picking coca, serving in the country's military and surviving, doing what he could to protect and provide for his family; I was and remain in robust admiration of him as a human being. I yearned for the chance to arrive in Tumaco to meet the rest of the family. We spent another day or two together in Cali and, on the final day of his trip, Jhon Jairo patted me on the shoulder, shook my hand, smiled and said, "*nos vemos por allá*, see you down there", and he was off to the bus terminal.

December in Colombia, especially in the sultry and bustling self-proclaimed world capital of salsa music that is Cali, is a festive time of year. Neighborhoods engage in an ongoing battle to see who can decorate their block with the best and brightest lights, painting different patterns or figures on the streets and sidewalks and, of course, the largest and loudest sound system possible. Music and motorcycles whirr through the streets regardless of the time of day; there is no avoiding the music. The actual Christmas celebrations with family and gifts takes place the evening of December 24th and there are multiple *navidad* anthems everyone from the older generations down to the children know the lyrics to. These songs are played in cafes, restaurants, shops, on radios in taxis and in the homes of people all throughout the city – everywhere a speaker is found.

As I arrived in Decepaz to spend Christmas with some of my biological family, the streets were alive with a variety of different rhythms. Within one block I heard salsa, reggaeton, cumbia and North American hip hop. Lights, large and small of varying bright colors, were strung everywhere, weaving in and out of bars protecting windows, wrapped around door handles, in between gates and resting on nails driven into wood or tubes jumping out from the brick and concrete – they were everywhere. Colorful streamers draped over doorways and gates, many next to or even on top of clothes hung out to dry in the evening breeze. Also, for Christmas, as well as New Year's Eve, people generally wear their best and newest clothes. My cousins dressed in their best but, while my feet were feeling better, I was still not ready to wear shoes. Flip flops, jeans and a button-up shirt were my choice for the evening. Throughout the night, I mingled with everyone I could, still very engaged in learning about my cousins and trying to learn the language. Close to midnight, we feasted on rice, chicken, ham and a mix of beer and aguardiente. There were a few neighbors down below beckoning for us to come out and dance, which we did for a few songs before retreating back up the ladder for a long, intoxicated conversation about the difference between celebrations in the States and Colombia.

A couple days later, I climbed onto a large bus with Ana, Leider, Milciades and Ana's sister-in-law Doris. We were headed to Tumaco on Colombia's southwestern Pacific coast to meet the rest of my biological mother's extended family. Ana reminded me the trip would last approximately fifteen hours. Our voyage would take us south all the way to the mountainous city of Pasto and then directly west to the coast. Almost completely filled, our bus pushed out of the busy streets in Cali southward towards Popayán. The bright green landscape of the Valle del Cauca gave way to the darker green and brown terrain of the Cauca department. Our bus winded up and down through small hills and tight turns, cutting through large pineapple fields on either side of the darkly paved road. Street vendors were at every gas station and every street restaurant or café, commonly wearing sports jackets, high black rubber boots, hats and ponchos.

A short time after passing through Popayán, the bus came to a slow stop. I was trying to take a nap but when I opened my eyes, soldiers were aboard the bus and began checking passengers' identification. At the time, military checkpoints were an inevitable part of moving between cities in a country still very engrossed by civil conflict. They were in place to keep the population safe, but they still made people uneasy, especially me since I was not accustomed to them. In addition, the only identification I had in my pocket, besides my U.S. driver's license, was a copy of my U.S. passport. I had not gone through the process of acquiring my Colombian passport or national identification yet. There was no real reason to be alarmed or uneasy at a Colombian military checkpoint. If we were to be stopped by the FARC or National Liberation Army (ELN) guerrilla groups, however, I heard many foreigners were being kidnapped and held for ransom. It was such an unlikely thing to happen that I immediately shook off the concern.

A soldier asked for my *cédula* (short for *cédula de ciudadanía*, Colombians' national ID) and I handed him the copy of my U.S. passport. He muttered something about needing to get my Colombian documents when I returned to Cali and ended with a short '*buen viaje*'. Because my U.S. passport indicates my place of birth, Colombian officials always demanded to see my Colombian documents. Ana handed him her ID, along with Doris and the boys'. His facial expression, a stern look of abject conformity to his position, remained unchanged as he moved from passenger to passenger. He moved without any hurry, shifting his weight slightly in his heavy boots, wearing a dark green uniform with a gun strapped to his hip. The mud he tracked onto the bus had a slight unique stench that I did not recognize, and his men grew increasingly impatient with how long it was taking to check all the IDs. Why they checked them and how exactly this process was meant to protect us, I will never know. Once their search was complete, the soldiers were off, and our bus continued on.

At this point on our trip, we reached a range of green lush mountains. We began to climb even higher into the Andean corridor and made our way to the chilly city of Pasto, capital of the Nariño department. It was dark outside, so I did not see much of the city as the bus jerked its way along narrow streets toward the bus terminal. The only thing I noticed was the difference in how the people looked once we left the Pasto bus station. Before, most of the people with us on the bus were white or mestizo, but after leaving Pasto, most of the passengers were black. I tried to remember the last time I had been on a bus with that many people of color and I could not recall a single occasion.

As we descended westward toward the coast, the areas surrounding Pasto were a gorgeous sight. The mountains gradually gave way to collection of rolling hills tropical vegetation. Scattered palm trees replaced extensive thick forest. Sunlight glinted off the highway and mist off in the distance announced a truly picturesque countryside. The humidity escalated inside the bus, but it did not dampen the mood. The atmosphere was lively. Many people laughed and yelled over each other in joyful conversation.

Suddenly, silent panic fell upon the bus as we slowed down once again. Audible gasps were heard from some passengers at the front of the bus. I glanced quickly at Ana to gauge her expression. Her eyes were fixed on something outside, yet she was not squinting. She pressed her lips together, let out a quick sigh and immediately started rummaging in her purse. I turned my head again to see what she was doing, and I saw her shove two cards into the folds of the seat between herself and Leider. "*No hable, oyó! Don't speak, did you hear!*" she instructed with a sharp whisper as her eyes jumped to the front of the bus.

I turned around from her and saw them at once, two men in uniform holding rifles with others outside the bus. The general feeling in the air was one of urgent consternation. The uniforms these men wore were somehow slightly different than those of the soldiers we had seen just south of Popayán. There were no last names to be seen anywhere on the uniforms either and no small Colombian flag on the shoulder. They also checked IDs in a different manner: they carried some kind of electronic scanner in their hands, at least one of them did, and he would put the *cédulas* into it for a few seconds before handing it back to the passengers. Then we were told to get out of the bus, with the women and children on the left side and the men on the other. As one of them holding a scanner walked down the line checking IDs, I wondered what I would say. I still did not know who these men were and what they would say once I showed them my U.S. passport copy.

When they came to me, I must have looked nervous because one of them said to me "*tranquilo, tu cédula por favor.* Relax, your cédula please." I handed him my passport copy and waited for the reaction. He smiled without showing his teeth then asked again for the cédula. I insisted, with my broken Spanish, that I did not have one yet. He paused, tilted his head to his right slightly and laughed again, his two partners at his side joining him. I will never know why he laughed or what he expected me to do in those seconds, but there was something eerie about the entire interaction. "*Disfruta Colombia, parce.* Enjoy Colombia, dude" he said with a raspy tone as he handed my passport copy back. His smirk lingered and his dark eyes seemed to pity me from under the shadow of his camouflage hat. He and his comrades continued to check other IDs, then, almost as soon as it had started, it was over, and we were told to get back on the bus quickly and leave.

For a few minutes after leaving the checkpoint, people were not really speaking. I reached for my red CD player just as Ana pulled at my hand. "*Eso no fue el ejército, Jake. Esa fue la guerrilla. Por eso escondí el carné escolar de los muchachos. Si ven que son hijos de un militar, hasta los pueden llevar*[16]*.*" I understood her perfectly and a hot sensation washed over my body. The unlikely event of being stopped by the FARC had indeed happened. I felt so naïve and yet, I was grateful for my ignorance for had I known whom I was talking to on the side of the bus, I may have not been able to hold my composure. I had studied the FARC and I knew what heinous acts they were responsible for at countless checkpoints similar to the one we had just driven away from, unscathed.

As we continued on, the highway eventually became less curvy and lush greenery sprouted up in all directions. In some spots, the trees and tall bushes were close enough to grab from the bus windows. The ride was smooth, the air felt thick and the sun beamed down on us. The occasional motorcycle sped past us. As I watched out my window, I was captivated by trees with colors and shapes I had never seen before. The few that looked

16 That was not the military, Jake. That was the guerrilla. That is why I hid the boys' school IDs. If the guerrilla see they're a military person's children, they could kidnap them.

familiar reminded me of trips to Maui. Off in the distance and through low-hanging fog, I saw short, wide palm trees. There were so many of them, and they grew in straight lines. Ana, sensing my curiosity, said proudly, "ésa es la palma africana. Ya estamos cerca de Tumaco, la tierra de tus ancestros[17]."

It was still morning when our bus finally reached the small bus terminal in Tumaco. My entire body ached from the long trip. The stress of being stopped by the FARC and the nervous excitement I felt about meeting the rest of the family left me exhausted. The bus terminal was so small that the larger busses did not even bother to enter. Instead, they parked on the street to load and offload passengers. I stepped out into the heat onto a street made of hexagonal concrete blocks covered by a light amount of sand that glimmered in the morning sun. The stench of fish and other seafood swirled around us while people scrambled to collect their bags and greet loved ones. As Ana and the others organized their things and we piled into a taxi, I noticed the buildings. They were short, mostly made of brick and concrete and were painted in a combination of dark and light tones. Zinc and concrete roofs were the norm. There were no taller structures at all which was a stark contrast to what I was accustomed to living in Cali. Indeed, the only tall things I noticed were three massive water towers off in the distance. Shops for clothing, shoes, fruits, meats, bars and other assorted establishments were everywhere. They were pressed tightly together and extended in every direction. Our cab moved quickly to the neighborhood, called La Comba, and we walked the narrow walkway between brick and wood homes toward our destination. Many of the neighborhood pathways

---

17 That is African palm. We are already close to Tumaco, the land of your ancestors.

were wide enough only for motorcycles to drive through. A few small children tagged along behind us, jumping and laughing.

A short, older woman with a dark complexion and black hair with a streak of gray running through it emerged from one of the single-story brick houses. She shuffled over to us, hugged Ana, then turned to me. She examined me closely and then smiled. "*Sé quien eres. Soy tu tía Nubia. Bienvenido a casa*! I know who you are. I'm your aunt Nubia. Welcome home!" Several children appeared at her side offering handshakes and hugs to welcome me. Looking at Nubia, I noticed some of the same features my uncle Ciro had, especially her nose and eyes. Her eyes had an identical sparkle. Within a few seconds of introducing herself, Nubia launched into an extensive apology. She explained, in slower language so I could fully understand her, how sorry she was for the condition she and rest of the family lived in. She apologized for being impoverished. She went on to say how she felt bad I was not coming to a "better neighborhood" with conditions that I was more accustomed to. She hugged me tightly and, in the formal form of the command for 'forgive us', she wailed, "*perdónenos*!" Unable to find the words for 'don't worry' in Spanish, I simply repeated "*no, no, no, todo está bien*. Everything is fine." Just then, another aunt appeared, and our small crowd grew larger. She was quiet; the many wrinkles in her dark forehead and under her deep eyes gave the impression I was standing before a wise woman. She extended her hand, looked me in the eye and introduced herself as my aunt Luz Dary. I returned the gesture with a tight hug and we all walked inside her house together.

Inside, I met her two young daughters Tania and Lucy, Lucy was affectionately called Firi, and son Daniel who everyone referred to as Dani, along with another sister, Yesenia, who was a bit closer to my age. I could not keep up with what was being said or even how to respond to the inundation of questions that came my way. The accent was going to take time to grow used to.

More and more family members continued to pour into Luz Dary's house to greet me. Neighbors also came from all around the neighborhood. I met my first cousins Jefferson, who everyone called Pulungo, Carlos also known as Calinga, Flavio and Yolima. I also met another uncle named Segundo, who, like my brother, was one of the fastest speakers I had ever met. After a series of warm greetings and more hugs, we took a short walk straight down the middle of the neighborhood to a wooden and brick home with seemingly no electricity. There, I was presented to my grandmother Lucila. She was a sweet old woman with patches of gray and white running through her hair. She squinted when she smiled and, once again, I noticed the same familiar facial features. It was inspiring to see she was still quite mobile and witty at her age, cracking jokes and telling the small children running around her to get out of her way or she would smack them with a machete. I could not tell if she was joking or not.

Aside from my overall awe of being surrounded by family, there were two things that stood out to me during those first couple of days in Tumaco. Primarily, I found it fantastically peculiar to be a member of the ethnic majority for the first time in my life. I did not see a white face anywhere I looked, and on some extraordinary level, I was calmed by that. Not because I harbored any sort of racist allegiance, but simply because I had never had that opportunity before. As far back as I could remember, I was always a minority in every social, athletic or academic setting growing up and as I transitioned to adulthood. However,

I did not speak to anyone about it, neither as I walked around in Tumaco, nor on the phone when I called my parents. This new sensation was for me to quietly savor alone, free of questions or judgement. There was nobody to challenge this sentiment, nobody to demand I justify my feelings. It was strangely uplifting. Sure, I was one of the lighter members of our family, but I still fit in. At the very least on the surface, I looked as though I belonged.

The second thing that struck me while in Tumaco, with my family for the first time, was the availability of water. It was treated as a true luxury. From my privileged perspective, using the bathroom quickly progressed into a well-calculated event rather than a routine pit stop. In my family members' homes, there was only one toilet and it did not flush. Instead, water from a nearby dark blue bucket, surrounded by swarming mosquitos, was poured in after each use to drain the bowl. Plastic buckets, large and small, were everywhere, but especially in close proximity to kitchens and bathrooms. There were no showerheads. In their place, larger buckets and tubs filled with rainwater sat inside or next to the place where the shower was. In order to bathe, a bar of soap was used to scrub oneself, and small bowls or cups were available to rinse using the rainwater from the larger tubs. Washing machines were scarce in the neighborhood which meant most people hand-washed their clothes in short, large plastic tubs while sitting on short wooden stools or bricks stacked atop one another. Throughout the neighborhood, clotheslines were strewn about donning freshly washed clothes dripping on the line or dry garments waving gently in the tropical breeze. Water ran beneath our feet in many of the narrow concrete pathways between the houses. In the middle of those paths, there were cement blocks and underneath them, drainage from homes in the neighborhood flowed through. Mosquitos took full advantage of the wastewater system and all other expressions of standing water. The very sweat on our foreheads, arms and legs ensured there was literally no escape from moisture in some fashion.

The biggest challenge with adjusting to my family's neighborhood was sleeping under mosquito nets. I tossed and turned my first night trying to sleep in Luz Dary's home, struggling to make sure the net stayed tucked beneath my small mattress. Even in the darkness I would catch occasional glimpses of them as they clung to the mesh netting that separated us, eager to plunge their tiny proboscis into my flesh. I remember counting thirty-eight of them one night, and those were only the ones I could see. Yet, despite this and other hindrances, Tumaco offered many positive things.

> *Miércoles 29 de Diciembre*
>
> *Tumaco is a paradise that inspires anyone who sets foot in its streets. Upon first impression, one might feel uneasy or perhaps a bit guilty at the sight of poverty, especially the wooden houses standing on sticks just out of the sea's reach. But underneath the poverty lies a population so friendly, so open and so happy. One arrives not knowing anyone but within half hour already has acquired at least two friends. Everyone seems to know each other on a first-name basis. The streets are well taken care of and you can tell people take pride in their small corner of the country.*

My family members were excited to show me the pride of Tumaco: the beach at El Morro. I heard from taxi drivers back in Cali about how much of a unique place it was. As we rolled up in Jhon Jairo's taxi, I caught my first sight of the beach, considered one of Colombia's main tourist attractions in the southwest part of the country. Palm trees greeted us as we stepped out onto the light gray sand and we walked toward a group of people playing music. My eyes found the Pacific Ocean and then the Peña El Quesillo rock formation, standing alone in the water, dotted with small trees and bushes. To the right of the Peña is an iconic rock wall formation stretching from the water's edge, all the way back along the beach toward the mangroves. This massive wall of limestone boasts a natural archway in the middle which acts as a gateway to other beaches and the vast ocean. Immediately in front of the archway is a natural wading pool. When the tide is high, countless children play tag and soccer in the knee-deep seawater of the tidepool. Seagulls, which I had not seen since leaving Washington State a few months before, glided in and out from under the archway, their shadows chasing each other on the wall of limestone, grasses and ferns. We set up a small soccer game using bottles and pieces of wood as our goal posts and my cousin Dani and I played against my brother and Leider. I am convinced we were victorious, although I do not actually remember the final score. The visual contrast of dark-skinned people backdropped by the light gray sand was quite a sight for me. I looked closely at the sand accumulating on my arms and legs and noticed flakes of a shimmering mineral that twinkled in the sun's reflection. People walking up and down the beach glimmered as they walked around, sparkling in the sun.

We stayed there all afternoon swimming, talking, listening to music and learning more about each other. I felt lost during most of the conversations and could not catch the majority of the jokes shared, but I did not care. I was there, precisely where I wanted to be. Tumaco earned a place in my heart as somewhere I could call home, a place I felt I belonged without fully understanding the linguistic colloquialisms or other cultural nuances. Tumaco also taught me, in an abrupt manner, to truly honor my North American socio-economic privilege I too often took for granted in ways Cali had not been able to. My parting gift from La Comba was a letter written in thin green Sharpie ink by my aunt Ana and with verbal help from various cousins and my other aunts.

Its translation is as follows:

Since October 26th, 2004 when we learned of your existence, we felt very happy, with a joy we do not fully know how to describe. We only knew that another member of our family existed, and he is a marvelous being. Thank you for coming to us and even though we are a humble family, we have the pleasure of being a united family and we receive you with all our heart. We give thanks to God because you came to give us one of the greatest joys we have had. Thank you for allowing us to enjoy some time with you and in that same light we give many thanks to your family for having taken you in and given you so much love, understanding and, above all, for making you such a human person and with such good morals. Thank you for being how you are and for having come to us. We hope to see you again very soon. We hope to continue in contact and knowing what you're up to from now on. Good luck, God bless you always. Your family who loves you very much.

On the other side of the same paper, I found the signatures of seventeen family members all neatly and vertically aligned. My grandmother, a few aunts and uncles, first cousins and my brother's signatures were all scribbled on the sheet. Each curve of the green Sharpie displayed a wide variety of handwriting. I pondered the significance of the letter, the signatures and the moment in general. The letter was only a collection of ten sentences but essentially it was a contract. As if my family members were saying, "we welcome you and now get ready to really be a part of this." The signatures formalized everything for me. Of course, there was no need to sign it with the pen but did so with my mind. As contracts go, there had to be some sort of obligation on my part. There was no way in that moment to know what exactly mine would be and I struggled to imagine what kinds of expectations would be bequeathed on me as the newest member of the family. Stepping into any new group inevitably elicits unspoken codes, rules and hopes for all parties involved. What were my new cousins, aunts and uncles expecting of me that they were not divulging between our hugs and laughs? What did I expect or hope of them?

My eyes did not leave the letter for the duration of the bus trip back to Pasto. I read the letter over and over as we made our way back to Popayán and eventually back to Cali, where I folded it and put it in my journal for safe keeping.

CHAPTER 7

The Silent Embrace

ON SUNDAY FEBRUARY SIXTH OF 2005, I WAS PICKING clothes off the ground in my room in our San Fernando house when I received the phone call about my biological mother. Daniela was on the phone with her mom when I heard her say she had another call coming in. "Mom, this is important, it's for Jake." When I picked up the phone, I heard my cousin Alejandra on the other end. She was frantic and instructed me to hurry to Decepaz because Deisy appeared again. Apparently, she was on her way to my uncle Vicente's house in the Mojica neighborhood and would be in a bus on her way to Decepaz shortly after. Alejandra believed I could intercept Deisy and she was convinced it would not be like the last time we tried at the hospital. It took me all of three minutes to change, grab my adoption documents and head out the door to hail a taxi.

I was familiar with the quickest routes from the San Fernando neighborhood to Decepaz both by taxi and by bus at that time. My talent for detecting accents from outside Cali had improved significantly as well, and I could tell my driver that day was from Pasto. He drove slowly and cautiously through the busy streets and I became annoyed since I was accustomed to Cali cab drivers' maniacal methods of navigating the streets. He missed a street that would have cut our arrival time significantly and I scolded him for it. When we finally arrived, he tried to charge me nearly double the usual amount to which I responded, "*jodéte,* fuck off", got out and ran to my uncle's house.

Almost immediately after arriving and talking with Alejandra for a few minutes, my aunt Ana called saying the people Deisy was with informed her they would be going to Ciudad Córdoba instead. Again, I was outside hailing a cab in the dusty street. I remained optimistic. By sharp contrast to my earlier taxi driver, this one arrived in fifteen minutes - a new record between Decepaz and Ciudad Córdoba. My heart pounded as I tossed my money at the driver and walked briskly to Ana's door without looking back.

Upon arrival, my cousin Leider informed me Deisy had not appeared yet. We sat to talk and watched Colombia become South American champions in the U-20 (athletes twenty years old and younger) regional soccer tournament while we waited. I glanced at the old clock on the wall multiple times and became more anxious as the game came to an end.

I started to succumb to the fearful reality that perhaps I was not going to meet this woman after all. I allowed myself to be seduced by the notion that meeting my biological family was enough — that I did not necessarily *need* to meet Deisy. I think this was in an effort to save myself from disappointment and also to protect my emotions. After all, my flight back to the Seattle area was only a few weeks away. At the very least, I had enjoyed an incredible seven months in Colombia including making meaningful progress with Spanish and meeting my biological family. Perhaps I would need to wait until my next visit to meet Deisy.

Leider and I decided to walk to the corner store for some Postobon soda and bread to celebrate Colombia's victory. The walk to the store and back took us approximately ten minutes and we took turns predicting how much it would rain as dark clouds hung overhead. As we approached the house's light brown steel door, Milciades jumped into the street screaming, "*Llegó, llegó Deisy*! She arrived, Deisy arrived!"

My feet stopped walking, as if somehow warning me not to continue, almost begging me to turn around and walk the other way. I was terrified because I wanted to make the best impression but did not know how. Perhaps I also did not know why. My legs grew weak, my clothes felt sodden with sudden sweat, yet I pushed past the entrance. My eyes adjusted to the dimly lit room, landing directly on a petite black woman standing to the left of the dining table. Ana, Leider and Milciades looked on, completely mute.

She stood with her tiny arms folded and she leaned so that most of her weight was on her right side. Her skin was dark and dry, tough like her fiery personality I had been warned of. The areas around her eyes as well as her cheeks twitched slightly behind her thick glasses and her jaw quivered as the first of many tears began to abandon her eyes. In that moment, words were incapable of freeing themselves from our lips. We were paralyzed as we stood in my aunt's living room, completely silent and embracing each other as twenty years hung nervously in the two or three inches of physical space that separated us.

Large tears cascaded down her face and found their way onto my left sleeve, soaking it almost completely.

> *Jueves 10 de Febrero*
>
> *I saw her right away...a tiny black lady with a red tank-top, black pants, glasses and small black hat that she made herself. Then came the hug. She kept crying and no tears came from me, even though I felt I could have cried for hours straight.*

As much as I wanted to, I found myself unable to cry, unqualified even. It was the only moment in my life when I really wanted to weep but could not. The failure to cry was a symptom of how I felt about this woman: wild elation for finally meeting her, deep pity for her physical state and, if I am honest, raw resentment. A large part of me wanted, or even needed, to hear her reasons for leaving me – why I was not worth fighting for. Twenty years. For twenty years she had kept me a secret from her entire family and, in this way, kept me from them. It seemed selfish to me. Twenty years of wondering about each other's existence and wellbeing. Twenty years of dreaming about each other. Twenty years' worth of questions. "*Mi hijo*!" she wailed, breaking the silence, wrapping her tiny arms and hands around my waist. I hugged tighter but also wanted to push her away; or did I push her away while wanting to hug her even tighter? My mouth was dry, and my eyes remained the driest they had ever been.

I tried frantically to consider what this meant for my immediate and distant future. This woman had unknowingly invaded every thought of mine since the day I learned of my adoption around six years of age. Every Mother's Day. Every birthday. She was the architect of all my curiosity regarding my biological family. She was also the villain whose reasoning for relinquishing me, I imagined, I would never forgive or understand and, admittedly, she was the queen atop the throne of my most naïve fantasies which I constructed on her behalf.

By this time, we were sitting side-by-side on my aunt's small mustard-yellow couch in the front room, her eyes still watery behind her glasses. Her miniature hands repeatedly attempted to block her tears from running down her face, but they were unsuccessful. I perceived she was an emotionally sensitive woman. Etched into her face were the wrinkles of a torn past. In her gaze I saw a lifetime of suffering - it was as if every time she looked up from crying, she was peering into the past and reaching desperately back to correct it. How many regrets did this woman have weighing on her brittle shoulders? Was I prepared to begin the process of peeling back those layers? Did she trust me? Could I love her and my adoptive mother equally or did I even have that right? Did one of them deserve more affection than the other? These are a handful of the questions that emerged as we sat trembling with uncertainty and a justifiable curiosity about each other's life.

Jueves 10 de Febrero

It is sad because I can hear her speak fine, but then I have to tell her things or respond to questions on paper. The first things that she said were asking me to forgive her for what she did, how she had no other options.

The following sentences exchanged between us caught me off guard, but I really had no idea of what to expect or say. There was no guidebook or manual on what to say to your biological mother who abandoned you and kept your birth a secret from her family. "*Tu papá.....tu papá se llama José Quiñones Ríos. Se parecen demasiado*[18]." She said, as her voice quivered. I was in no way prepared for those words. She held her hands together on her knees and she stared at the blank wall in front of us. My biological father?

In all the years that transpired I thought only about her and had not allowed myself to wonder about the life of this man. This new piece of information occupied my mind like a swarm of ferocious wasps.

I was momentarily frozen and then remembered the copies of the adoption documents in my bag. I passed her a note which read, *QUIERO MOSTRARTE ALGO Y PODEMOS HABLAR*[19]. Reaching for the documents, I imagined what her reaction might be. She was about to be confronted about her decision to leave me and possibly never imagined this day would come; or maybe she had. Either way, I believed it was my right to know her reasons and I felt my hands and forehead take on a renewed anxious sweat. In the collection of papers, there is one key sentence I have clung to since reading them at the orphanage years before: "since the third month of pregnancy, señora María Deisy Mosquera decided to give her child in adoption." As she held them, I watched carefully as her dark eyes darted from side to side as she read. Her brow wrinkled and her mouth

18 Your father...your father's name is José Quiñones Ríos. You two look a lot alike.

19 I want to show you something and we can talk.

morphed into a deep frown. The paper trembled in her hands and suddenly she ripped the page to pieces shouting "*mentiras! Son puras mentiras*! Lies! They are all lies!"

The pieces fell to the floor and she buried her face in her hands, sobbing and wailing at the same time. What caused such a reaction? What could I say? Lies? I was in shock. No amount of advice or other psychological preparation could have prepared me for what she described next.

When she regained her composure, she turned to me, pausing slightly as she wiped her eyes and adjusted her glasses. She cleared her throat, put her right hand on my left knee and said slowly and sternly, "*nunca te regalé. Qué tipo de madre haría eso*[20]*?*" She continued to remove her glasses to wipe her tears, but they kept coming. So many scars covered her arms. Her jaw was crooked and quivered constantly. Her lack of hearing meant that when she spoke, she could not recognize when a syllable or accent need to be stressed and she spoke in quick, high-pitched bursts; but I could understand everything. She went on to describe her rare bone disease which was, I later learned, a condition called osteogenesis imperfecta. She revealed the C-section scar from which I emerged and described the numerous visits she had made to the hospital and clinics all around the city throughout her life. Her voice and hands trembled, telling me about her ear infections that led to her eventual hearing loss, the many times she slipped and fractured her bones in the street or the two times she had been hit by a car. Since that very day, she has been hit on one more occasion. In her right leg, she had a steel rod running parallel to her femur. Metal pins were inserted in her jaw and a few more in her right arm. All of this,

20 I never gave you up. What kind of mother would do that?

plus crushing poverty and almost complete voluntary isolation from her family meant she was, and continues to be, a woman who suffers through every aching minute of life. It was like she was leading me on a tour of all the reasons to feel sorry for her, and it was working.

> *Jueves 10 de Febrero*
>
> *She kept telling me how she had suffered her whole life. She showed me her legs as proof, and I felt like crying. They bent in ways I never knew to be possible. She explained everything about how the doctors told her she could not have a normal birth because of her bones...so they did the C-section. Then how they asked her: how can you support this baby when you cannot support yourself? She was the perfect picture of sadness and with each word and through her tears, I became sadder for her. It was if she had forgotten how to smile.*

There came a point in our discussion when I found myself yearning to leave. A thousand thoughts and questions about my biological father ran wild around my head, but they were not what disturbed me most. What truly burned and made me feel nauseous was the thought that I could have been taken from my biological mother. The rage she displayed when holding the copies of the adoption documents was very real. It was raw, and still, from the look on her face, very fresh in her mind.

The thought of being stolen launched me into a severe existential predicament. The simple story that had accompanied me since childhood was some version of the classic "your biological mother could not provide for you so.... here you are." Never had the idea about being taken from her crossed my mind because it never needed to. This conversation never arose with my parents, teachers, family members, therapists or friends. This woman had been through so much, cried so many tears and hurt for so long; and I enjoyed such unfading privilege! As it had before, guilt about my privileged upbringing compared with her constant struggles returned to choke me. Yet, I felt all credit was due to Deisy for making the decision that would eventually make that privilege possible for me. Right? Or credit due to my parents back in the States for providing a nurturing home? I was confronted with the following unsettling question: was I truly abandoned and, if not, what or who was responsible for ensuring it looked that way? My mind was awash with so many things that all that seemed reasonable was to flee the scene.

> *Jueves 10 de Febrero*
>
> *By that time, it was actually becoming hard for me to be there sitting by her side as she wept. I kept thinking what I could do to make her feel better but then I became discouraged when she said that she did not know why she was still alive. So, we walked out to the corner of Ana's street, hugged and I was gone.*

There I was, having finally achieved what I imagined to be impossible and what countless other adoptees around the world seek out during the course of their lives, and all I wanted to do was sprint across the city without looking back. A pounding headache rattled my skull. With identical fury as when I arrived hours before in the taxi, I was now hurrying out the door, retreating back into the humid chaos of the street. The familiar chorus of car horns, busses, motorcycles, music and children's shouting soothed me after spending the afternoon enduring extended moments of deafening silence. My body ached and longed for a frigid shower back in San Fernando. I needed a couple days to process, to reflect, to plot my next move in this one-player chess match my life had evolved into.

Four days later, I was sitting with Deisy in the house of Ms. Rosa, a woman she previously provided domestic services to, in Ciudad Córdoba. We were at a large oak table with my journal and other pieces of notebook paper spread out while smells of onions and beef swirled around us as dinner was prepared. I left the journal with Deisy when we met at Ana's and requested she write down what happened with me as a baby and why. She accepted, and we were meeting again to go over it together. Here is the translation of what she wrote:

Dear Jake of my heart, I want to write to you to clear up all your concerns, since you have the right to know the truth. I worked at a family's house in the Santa Teresita neighborhood and that is where I met your father, José Quiñones Ríos. He lived five blocks from where I worked. We were dating for about five months, he taught in a school in the area. He said he needed to go to Pereira, he tried to get me to go with him, I could not. About a month after he did, I started to have pains and vomiting. I went to the doctor and he said I was pregnant. I searched for your father, but I could not find him. I stopped working by order of the doctor because I was in danger of losing you. When I met your father, I already had a year and a half working but I did not have money. With loans from people, I survived on my own for the full nine months. God knows I wanted to have you because the short time I spent with your father was very nice. I wanted to keep a memory of him by having you. He was a very special man. He loved kids and he was very caring and well educated like you. My son, you look very much like him in every way. We understood each other very well. I never had anyone by my side like your father.

I passed the nine months in the Mariano Ramos neighborhood. When the time came to have you, I went to the Carlos Carmona Hospital which is close to Mariano Ramos. The doctor told me they had to operate on me, that I could not have a normal birth because everything was very inflamed. They sent me to the Department Hospital. There you were born April 3rd, 1984. The next day, a social worker named Olga Andrade came to my bed. She asked questions like where I lived, why I was alone, I told her many things. She responded by saying "because of the conditions you are in, you cannot take the baby yet. How will you feed him? You do not have a job and you are paying rent; the baby does not have any clothing. Let's do the following: I will take the baby to Bienestar Familiar while you recuperate a bit. He will be well taken care of. When you're in better conditions, go to Bienestar Familiar to get him." I trusted too much in that woman. She did not even give me any contact information. I told her your name was Andres Felipe. You were sleeping next to me and from there she took you. I never saw that woman again. Five days later I went to the hospital and asked to see you, but people told me no because I was still in bad conditions. The C-section was approximately 15cm and it hurt a lot even to walk. After two weeks I went to the hospital and searched for the social worker and again they told me I was not fully recuperated. I waited another ten days to go back and they told me that woman no longer worked at the hospital. I went to Bienestar Familiar and they told me there had not been any social worker from the Department Hospital and definitely not with a newborn baby. That is where my agony began, searching in the hospitals and Bienestar Familiar. I never knew what had happened to you. That's why I left everything in God's hands, and I kept everything from my family. They have never supported nor helped me in anything. I have been sick, sometimes with long times being hospitalized, and they, knowing I was there, never went to visit me. I always suffered in silence without having anyone to share my sadness. There were only a few friends who would be with me crying while I asked where my son could be. What was he eating or was he in the street? It got to the point where I would see children in the street asking for money and wonder if they were you. In this moment I would give my life to pull out that resentment you carry in your heart. God is my witness that everything I have told you is true. I never took you to an adoption center. I always asked myself why that woman left the hospital and why the document describing your medical history disappeared. And how now, with the documents you showed me, there is a social worker report that says I left you. I assure you those papers are falsified. They took information from your medical history.

I want to tell you that just as the lord made the miracle of getting to know about you and meet you after twenty years, here I will wait until my last days to clear up everything. Now I have no doubts that you were stolen. You were a healthy and cute baby. The doctors told me that. I also want to tell you that because I was so poor, I left everything in God's hands since I did not have the money to pay a lawyer.

Naturally, I believed everything she wrote as undisputable fact. I trusted her because, as I asked myself over and over again sitting at that table, what did she stand to gain by lying to me? The idea of being stolen from her consumed me. Finding out her original plan for my name intrigued me. She paused suddenly, wiped her mouth with a napkin, and asked who named me Alfonso. I had no idea. For Deisy, that was more than enough confirmation to suspect some kind of wrongdoing in my adoption process. Then, in a demonstration of how quickly her mood could shift, she poked fun at the name. For the first time, she tried to joke with me, saying that the name Alfonso was for "*viejitos con barrigas de cerveza!* Old men with beer bellies!" I laughed began to contemplate different ways to try and make her smile.

> *Jueves 10 de Febrero*
>
> *She laughed a few times. In her own way and jaw-permitting, but she laughed. It was more like a soft squeak, but it was enough for me. We ate some more beans and rice that Rosa prepared and then it was time to leave. But before leaving and after saying goodbye to Rosa, Deisy gave me the address and telephone number where she was living. Nobody else in the family or the world had that information—just me. So, I had earned her trust and in that, she gained mine.*

We ate at the table slowly and, just as with Jhon Jairo two months earlier, she spent the meal asking me about my life. What were my parents like? Who were my best friends? What did I do in my spare time? We talked about favorite sports, colors, foods, music, my studies, travels, sister and my goals for the near future.

It is a colossal understatement to claim I did not feel mentally prepared to return to the US. There were so many things that needed to be finished. I was only beginning to feel confident having full conversations in Spanish and, above all, I really wanted to continue getting to know Deisy and the rest of the family. I felt it was unfair to be leaving her so soon.

The afternoon I said goodbye to her, we hugged for nearly as long as we did when we met. We promised each other to email as frequently as possible. Then, as I walked towards the door, we paused for one more hug and I was off.

CHAPTER 8

Disillusionment

MY PROMISE TO THE FAMILY IN CALI AND TUMACO was to return to Colombia every two years for a brief visit. The summer of 2007 was my chance to honor that promise and I was ecstatic to get back and pick up where I left off. I had one main objective for the trip: establish a more profound connection with Deisy. A handful of friends and my aunt Ana offered to host me, but I thought the best way to really get to know my biological mother was to live with her for the full two months of my visit. Through our sporadic email correspondence over the course of the two years since seeing each other, I knew she lived with and worked for a family from Tumaco who lived in the northern part of Cali, and they were ready and willing to have me stay with them.

It was my first trip to Colombia completely alone and I felt prepared to take on the challenge. I would not have the luxury of relying on Daniela or Gloria for advice or tips this time. Everything was going to be up to me, and I was not afraid.

Deisy's employers, Jesús, Miriam and their family, immediately made me feel at home in the Guaduales neighborhood. The house was a one-story dimly lit home with white painted cement walls, white and gray floor tiles and mostly wooden furniture. Multiple decorations were navy blue. Their three daughters, Samara, Karen and Mariuxi lived with them, as well as Karen's daughter, Nicol and Mariuxi's son, Jhosua. Including Deisy and myself, there was a total of nine sharing one bathroom, two small bedrooms, a kitchen and common space with a beautiful oak dining table.

Colombian hospitality is a serious endeavor. Afro-Colombian hospitality, by comparison, is so serious it even approaches being austere. Jesús flatly rejected my insisting that someone else take the bed I was assigned. It did not feel right that I just got off the plane, met these welcoming people for the first time ever, and was instantly given a full bed to myself. Everyone else in the house, including the children, had to find other spaces to lay their heads at night. I did nothing to deserve such generous treatment.

One morning, as I began to familiarize myself with the Guaduales neighborhood, and reacquaint myself with the bus routes, Deisy said she wanted to talk. We sat down outside in the sun, mosquitos rushing to join us. She held a beat-up, small black briefcase and squeaked, "we need to talk about some things." I nodded with raised eyebrows as she unzipped the bag. Her little hands frantically began taking out paper after paper, nearly all of them with underlined, highlighted and circled information marked in black, blue and red ink. I peered at a few of them and found each page was a different email exchange between us. She printed every email message from the time we met in early

2005 up to mid 2007. I could not believe it. Each page had large circles over some sentences, others were crossed out. More than a few pages were torn in half, others rippled from exposure to rain. What exactly did she wish to achieve by looking at these pages with me?

"*Por qué me odias*? Why do you hate me?" she asked, her eyes fixated on a little boy kicking a ball against a cement wall a few meters in front of us, the papers strewn about between us. I was furious. How dare she accuse me of such a thing. What sense did it make for me to hate her when I did everything in my power to find her and work toward building a lasting relationship with her? I wasted no time in grabbing the pen by my side, flipping over one of the papers and scribbling madly on the blank side. I wrote so quickly that the words were not legible, and I had to start over. I was set on not actually answering her question since I truly did not hate her. It seemed ridiculous. Instead, I demanded she provide evidence for her outrageous claim. When I was finished, I thrust the paper into her hands, folded my arms across my chest and waited for her response. I did not even want to look at her while she read. I felt the need to contemplate all the ways I was offended by her question.

I finally looked at her and saw the familiar sight of tears rolling down her face from behind her glasses. She shook her head back and forth repeatedly, without saying anything. A few seconds went by before she motioned with her right hand toward all the papers and said slowly, "Look at the papers. The evidence you want is all there." I looked through them, searching for anything in my typed words that could be perceived as rude or disrespectful. I came to one question that stated, "*y cómo está toda la familia por allá*[21]*?"* This particular question was circled many times in red ink. I turned to her, pointed to it and waited for her response. "You know I do not talk very much to the family. So, you choose to mock me. It is very disrespectful." I was dumbfounded. From my perspective, the email was simply asking, in the most genuine way possible, how the family was doing. When we met in 2005, she expressed a desire to "repair the scars with the family" and I recall trying to encourage her to do so.

We sat there for approximately two hours as I tried to explain, through writing on the back of the printed emails, my thoughts behind each circled paragraph from months and even years prior. It was a completely futile exercise for me, and I lost patience having not even completed half of the task Deisy set out for me. For the first time, I lied to her and said I needed to go meet some friends in another part of the city. I really had no idea where I would go, I just knew I needed some space.

We picked up the papers and Deisy placed the brief-case under my bed, telling me that we would continue looking through them another time. I nodded, gave her an insincere hug and turned to walk out the door.

The bustling seventieth street was always filled with busses. Being one of the busiest streets in the northern part of the city, one could catch a bus anywhere. I decided to go to the Parque del Perro in the San Fernando neighborhood to see how it changed since living there with Daniela and Lucía. I jumped onto a bus, found a seat next to a dental student fumbling her textbooks and breathed a sigh of relief, even with all the car horns and chaos around me.

---

21 And how is all the family over there?

Once at the corner of fifth and thirty-fourth street, I made my way westward into the Parque del Perro. There was a pleasant afternoon breeze as I got my first glimpse of the park since leaving two years prior. Some of the shops and small restaurants changed and the internet café I always called my parents and friends from was no longer there. As I turned to scan the rest of the park, I noticed a small black woman move behind a car, clearly trying to avoid being seen. I waited and then she stuck her head out - it was Deisy. I never saw her on the bus, so I concluded she followed me in a taxi. Our eyes met for a split second and she turned abruptly to walk in the opposite direction, back toward fifth street. The thought of running to ask why she followed me never crossed my mind. I turned to walk the other way as well and I seethed for the next few moments. To my knowledge, nobody ever followed me before. More than hurt, I was livid and felt my privacy was violated. How ironic that it was by the woman I had searched so hard for! This cemented a disturbing realization for me: Deisy did not trust me and this surely would contribute to the continued deterioration of our relationship. I had told her I was going to see friends, yet I was walking in a park, alone, with nothing but a small backpack and water bottle in my possession. We both lost considerable trust in each other that humid afternoon. All of this clouded my mind as I saw her tiny frame waddle out of sight into the blur of palm trees, motorcycles and busses.

I returned to Jesús and Miriam's house that night with no intention of asking Deisy why she followed me. Instead, I decided to not acknowledge what transpired and opted to eat and speak with Miriam. She was curious to learn more about what life in the U.S. was like, especially for black people. As we sat talking in the main room, drinking some water, Deisy worked tirelessly in the kitchen preparing a dish. Scents of chicken, cilantro and onions filled the house. The other family members joined us as we sat at the table to enjoy a late dinner. My favorite juice from the lulo fruit was passed around in a large tin container. The meal was good, but I did not finish because I ate a large meal in the street before arriving back at the house. I ate about half of my plate before getting up to put the rest of the food, that I had not touched, back in the large pot it came from. I caught a glimpse of Deisy peering at me and shaking her head, her glasses reflecting the low kitchen light.

She was at my side almost immediately as I walked into the bedroom to get some flip flops, pinching my right arm and pulling me down to speak into my ear. "You lie to my face. You are ungrateful and you do not appreciate the food I make. Eres un mal hijo. You are a bad son." Her declaration stung. She was correct about the lie. I lied to her face. But, the part about being ungrateful and being a bad son really offended me since I felt it was blatantly untrue. I wanted to respond, but I had no words. She was back out with the family helping in the kitchen and acting as though nothing happened. I decided not to respond. Instead, I pulled up a chair next to Jesús to talk about soccer and Colombian politics. I went to sleep early that night trying to focus on what lay ahead. Luckily, I was about to get a brief reprieve from the growing tension with Deisy.

The following afternoon, I leaped into another taxi with excitement because I was going to meet someone special for the first time. At least, it was going to be the first meeting as an adult. I was on my way to see Isabella Sinisterra, the woman who, twenty-three years earlier, cared for me during my time at

Chiquitines prior to my adoption. We exchanged emails before I arrived in the country and I knew meeting her would be the highlight of my trip.

In our messages, I learned Isabella was acquainted with Agatha, the director at Chiquitines. They ran into each other at a birthday party in 2005, and Isabella asked Agatha if she knew anything about a baby named Alfonso Mosquera a baby she cared for and wanted to adopt in the 1980s. She told Agatha about how, as a student and volunteer at the orphanage, she used to care for him and took him many times to be with her parents and extended family to their house in the south of the city, as well as a family farm outside of the city limits on several occasions. Agatha was shocked by their connection and delighted to tell Isabella I just finished living in Colombia for almost eight months. She gave her my email address and Isabella wrote to me that same night.

I stepped out of the taxi into bright sunlight and oppressive heat at the entrance of the Cali Zoo, where Isabella was attending a music workshop for a youth group she volunteered for. She emerged wearing a bright red t-shirt, jeans and a smile I recognized from some pictures my mom showed me of her when I was little. My mom only remembered her by her first name, María, and I remember as a child promising my mom I would meet María someday. And there we stood, locked in an embrace at the zoo, twenty-three years later and just down the street from where the original Chiquitines orphanage was located. Her eyes welled up and she repeatedly exclaimed how excited she was. She was light in complexion with sharp features, hazel eyes and dirty blonde hair that extended just beyond her shoulders.

As she wiped her eyes, her voice trembled as she shouted, "*cuéntame todo! Qué has hecho con tu vida*[22]*?*" I filled her in with the basics of studies, jobs, friends and my family back in the U.S. Our steps were slow as we walked toward her car, chatting about everything as if we had known each other for years. Isabella had such a calming presence. I felt comfortable speaking to her even if I was spewing grammatical nonsense.

We drove to her condominium, which was not very far from the zoo, and I was overwhelmed with how luxurious it was. Hers was one of multiple condo and apartment buildings in that area, all with at least ten floors, some made of concrete and others of elaborate brick designs. Exotic plants and trees decorated the common spaces of the building and when we walked into her condo, I was greeted by her ex-husband and her son, Juan Antonio. As I sat, engaged in small talk with all of them, I could not stop comparing their lifestyle to that of the family Deisy and I were staying with, and simultaneously, to that of my biological family. The floors were made of elegant tile, the furniture matched impeccably, and various ceramic and acrylic artworks decorated every available space. The balcony overlooked the busy Santa Teresita neighborhood and we could see all the way to the downtown area and toward the north of the city.

I wanted to spend more time with Isabella and express how grateful I was to her taking care of me all those years before; but our conversation was cut short because they needed to be somewhere. I needed to get back myself to try to mend things with Deisy. We decided we would meet another day, just the two of us, to spend a large part of the day together. We hugged, I took

22 Tell me everything! What have you done with your life?

down all her contact information and I was out the door, down the elevator and back into the heat.

Walking back into Jesús and Miriam's house in Guaduales, Deisy wasted no time demanding to know where I had been and with whom. I grabbed a piece of paper to write down the story of Isabella and sat with her on the couch for an hour to explain everything. She nodded repeatedly, seemingly in approval. Suddenly, she hugged me, almost aggressively, and shrieked "I am happy you have good people in your life. Good job, keep her close." I did not expect that reaction from her, but I also allowed myself to feel warmed by her upbeat shift in attitude. She yanked at my shirt, pulling me closer to her on the couch, and kissed me on the cheek, giggling slightly. While confusing, the rare light-hearted moment was more than welcome. I let myself be seduced by the idea of repairing her trust and kept my mom's words of wisdom ever-present: "remember, she is trying to make up for twenty-plus years of not knowing you."

I awoke a couple days later to the hurried sounds of someone struggling with a zipper, directly underneath my bed. I kept my personal belongings in a small backpack there. Inside were a couple books, socks, underwear, two smaller notebooks exclusively for communication with Deisy, some money and my U.S. passport. It was very early in the morning, still dark, and as I sat up, I heard a gasp and noticed the silhouette of someone jump back abruptly. I switched on the small light to my left and saw Deisy standing motionless, her back against the wall and both her hands frozen behind her back. I could see sweat gathered on her brow and glistening in the lamp light, her eyes set on the ground between us. I knew I caught her doing something suspicious and that she was hiding something behind her back. Her body language indicated she was ashamed or maybe just angry at having been caught. I seized the black pen lying next to the lamp and scribbled the following on a napkin: QUÉ NECESITAS? ESTÁS BIEN[23]? I held it up in front of her, now sitting up fully in the bed. Upon reading, her eyes returned to the ground and her jaw quivered. She continued to shake her head as I sat still holding the message.

Finally, she flung her arms out from behind her back and my passport was on the floor. She buried her face in her hands and tried to comfort herself with her tears. I was perplexed. I bent down to pick up my passport, put it on the nightstand wrote another message: POR FAVOR EXPLÍCAME POR QUÉ NECESITAS MI PASAPORTE[24]. Again, she responded with more tears and head shaking. My patience expired moments before, but I was acting out of pure curiosity. The napkin was filled with words, so I switched to one of the small blue notebooks, pressing her to explain why she tried to take my passport while I was sleeping. I assured her I would not get angry with her (which of course was a blatant lie, I was furious). After about ten minutes of my pleading she realized I was not going to let it go. She sat down next to me on the bed with a defeated sigh. Early morning light was just starting to show itself through the windows and she grabbed my right hand, still unable to look at me. She did not whisper, but she did her best not to raise her voice as she explained that she knew I needed a passport to leave the country. She mumbled the verb *quemar* and something about my passport. I wrote for her to repeat what she said, she hesitated, then finally did as I requested. It took me a few seconds but then

---

23 What do you need? Are you alright?

24 Please explain to me why you need my passport.

I recalled the translation of *quemar* is 'to burn'. Deisy continued to explain her plan to burn my passport in order to keep me in the country. This way, she continued, I would need to stay in Cali and buy her a house.

It was not her warped sense of logic that frustrated me, nor was it the fact she woke me up in the early morning. My skin crawled with rage because of what I perceived to be completely wicked audacity. How dare she! Who did she think I was? Who was she, really? I wanted to grab my bags and run out the door. Instead, I calmed my body and wrote carefully that I could not buy her a house and asked if we could talk about it later after I got some more sleep. She read, nodded, kissed my hand and retreated to the laundry room. I stayed awake, alternating between staring at the ceiling and the wall Deisy leaned against with my passport behind her back. How foolish I was to believe we were on our way to rebuilding trust. Did she not know how she was making me feel or have any concept of the consequences of her actions? Either she simply did not or, more disturbingly, she opted not to care. And if she really did not care, then what the hell was I still doing staying with her? What did I hope to accomplish, other than giving her more opportunities to disrespect and take advantage of me? I chewed my fingernails violently as I contemplated my next move. I needed to find another place to stay. The tension between Deisy and me was too fierce to continue at the Guaduales house, even if Jesús and Miriam were gracious hosts.

I was at a mental crossroads. I was overjoyed to be spending so much time with Deisy. It was a fantastic culmination of years of curiosity and unanswered questions, finally being unraveled before my eyes. However, the selfish and immature side of me wanted more. The truth was simple: Deisy did not live up to the fantasy I created about her over the course of my life. My hope was that she would be an upstanding citizen, committed to her family, hard-working and with some level of higher education. Of course, it was not fair of me to claim that she was not hard-working or an upstanding citizen, whatever that meant. But I had expectations of what I hoped and wanted her to be. Deep down, I wanted to be proud of her, to claim her. I wanted to take pictures to put on my refrigerator back home and say to friends and family alike, "See that? That is my biological mother in Colombia. She is fantastic." In my confusion and disappointment, this broken, defeated and alienated little woman who sat before me was not worthy of such praise. How I wished someone, another adoptee, friend or family member would have told me to keep my expectations for meeting her low. It would have been logical, even nice. The reality is, those warnings probably did come in droves. But I could not, would not pay attention to them. If loved ones did warn me against falling for my own preconceived notions of what Deisy would be like, I do not remember any of it. It was the harshest of lessons. I was forced to realize the idea of her eclipsed who she was in reality and it tore me up inside. This new episode of mistrust left me scrambling to get on a bus and head south to Tumaco to escape the tension and clear my head.

Due to news reports of guerrilla and paramilitary presence along the southern highway connecting the cities of Pasto and Tumaco, I decided it was not safe to take a bus there. Instead, I purchased a roundtrip plane ticket with the small Satena airline company to take a five-day trip. I would have stayed in Tumaco longer, but I really wanted to spend more time getting to know Isabella and other friends from years before.

Flying to Tumaco from Cali cut the trip from roughly fifteen hours to forty-five minutes and offered spectacular views of the southwestern part of the country as it met the tranquil blue of the boundless Pacific Ocean. At the scanty La Florida airport, whose black runway rests in the middle of a large field surrounded by lanky and petite palm trees, I hopped into the first taxi I saw and instructed the driver to take me to my family's neighborhood.

Because of my recent difficult interactions with Deisy, the next few days and evenings were spent contemplating how to move forward and also to try and learn more about her background from my aunts and uncles who knew her best. I hoped to further understand why she acted the way she did and if I was the only one enduring such negative treatment from her. Between battling mosquitos and conversing extensively with extended family members, my main question evolved into what they would do in my situation. Most all of them replied I should distance myself from her since I certainly was not gaining anything by trying to understand how her mind worked. I nodded in silence, taking mental notes. The continued deluge of disparaging remarks about Deisy made me feel uneasy. It was a mixture of anger and acquiescence. Part of me wanted to defend her, to stand up for her to her siblings. However, I kept quiet. My silence felt like an endorsement for them to keep making fun of her. Persistent warnings from relatives rained down on me about how I needed to be wise and not end up like her – as if she had somehow made a series of conscious decisions to choose her misfortune. None of those voices rang more forcefully to me than that of my grandmother, Lucila, known locally as 'doña Lucha'.

When I peered into her home at the end of the narrow concrete corridor of the neighborhood, it was almost completely dark aside from a dim lamp off in the corner of her one-room abode. The smooth cement floor was cool to the touch as I sat down to have my first one on one conversation with her. She sat on a short block of wood, no more than six inches high, and wore a black skirt made of a thin material with images of white flowers on the bottom. Her blouse was a flawless white and a thin gold necklace hung around her neck. Matching hoop earrings swung slightly as her right hand jostled back and forth while she peeled a coconut with a rusty machete without a handle.

"Your mother has always caused me problems. Since she was little, I always had to have a strong hand with her", she said without looking up from the coconut. It was like she knew precisely why I was paying her a visit. She mumbled something else and I asked her to repeat herself.

"I said I think it is best to focus your attention on spending time with the family. Deisy will not appreciate or value you. She does not appreciate or value anyone. It is very sad."

She continued peeling her coconut, being careful not to bring the machete blade too close to her bare feet. She grunted with each chop of the blade and insisted we talk later that evening when she noticed I had not moved. It was clear to me the unilateral conversation had reached its end only moments after it had begun. There was so much I wanted to ask, so much more I wanted to ask Lucila about her own upbringing, about her siblings, about everything. But it was not to be. I never even earned her eye contact as I sauntered out from her house and back through my aunt Nubia's wooden door.

The other couple of days in Tumaco were spent rotating between my two aunts' houses in search of conversations reaching beyond the superficial. Unfortunately, my listening comprehension skills were still ill-equipped to follow conversations occurring around me in the thick Tumaco accent. Most of the time I sat listening to cousins, aunts and uncles as they laughed hysterically, their laughter ringing out through windows and into the street. I never understood any of the jokes. Passersby shouted greetings from the suffocating heat, shifting their feet slowly to the rhythms of motorcycles engines and salsa music. My last night I invited my brother and some cousins out to a bar for some drinks and dancing. The following morning, Jhon Jairo whisked me to the airport on his motorcycle and before I knew it, I was back at the airport in Cali plotting my next move.

As I stepped off the bus back in the Guaduales neighborhood, I knew I could not stay with Deisy in the same house anymore. Realizing this felt like I was giving up on her and I did not know how to feel about it. I felt sad for her because surely her actions were not completely intentional. Or maybe she just really had no idea how to understand the consequences of her actions. It was very possible she felt powerless against my perceived condescending mannerisms as her spoiled American son. I began to think that I could be the one to blame for all the tension and mistrust. Either way, staying with her at the house was no longer an option.

I knocked on their door and little Nicol opened it to let me in. I had grown quite close with the kids and their mothers during my brief time with them. I walked to each member of the family and told them, without lengthy explanations, that I needed to go stay with some friends for my last week-and-a-half of my trip in Cali. Miriam, whom I had also grown quite close to, let out a long sigh and said she understood why I needed to leave. She urged me to do what I could to repair the mistrust between Deisy and I.

Deisy was sitting on the bed when I walked in to start packing my bags. She jumped to hug me and started peppering me with questions about my short visit to Tumaco. I responded with toothless half smiles and nodded or shook my head to each question, which mostly had to do with the sons and daughters of my cousins. I sat down on the bed, grabbed a piece of paper and began to write. She sat down to my right, leaning over slightly to get a better view of what I was telling her. She folded her arms as I wrote about needing to go stay with friends in the southern part of the city and immediately demanded the address of where I would stay. She insisted she needed the information in case she needed to contact me in the event of an emergency. Anticipating she would try to follow me again, I made up an address in the southern-most part of the city. I wrote a fake street number and a fake building number. The only thing that actually existed was the neighborhood, named Ciudad Jardín. To travel from Guaduales to Ciudad Jardín is to travel from the northern extreme of the city to the southernmost tip and requires spending significant time in a bus if you cannot get there in a private car or taxi. I knew this and I still opted to send her in that direction if she indeed plotted to try to follow me. I felt bad but I also felt I had no other choice. Deisy studied the address and declared she knew how to get there. I shrugged. Then she asked for the phone number, so I wrote down a false house number. She requested my friend's name and I said no, citing a desire to respect their privacy even though I had just divulged this fake person's contact information.

My bags were packed and ready, so I stood up and thanked my hosts again before stepping into the street. Deisy insisted on seeing me to the bus stop and I quickly devised a plan to ensure she could not follow me. At the bus stop, we hugged for a few moments and I looked at her. It was painfully obvious this was the last time I would see her during my trip. I was relieved, almost celebratory, that I would not see her until my next time in Colombia, and I had no idea when that would be. I knew it would be a couple of years.

I pulled away from her grasp, walked onto the bus and sat down with my things. We drove away and the relief I felt was greater than I expected. I was weary to not give in completely to that feeling. The bus reached a stop closer to downtown and I got off, walked two blocks and boarded a different bus, with a completely different route, and headed eastbound toward the Distrito Aguablanca. That bus came to a stop after about ten minutes and again, I walked off with my things. I was going to make it impossible for Deisy to follow me and I could not stay put so I hailed a cab. My instructions for the driver were to take me to the Parque del Perro, and off we went, fully westbound. Once at the park, I had some ice cream and caught another taxi which took me to the Hotel Residencia Stein, my final destination and the same place my mom stayed with her friends a few years earlier on her trip to surprise me. I knew they would have a room available and I also knew that if Deisy managed to follow me, she would need to ask the hotel guards to be let past the gates and into the lobby area. I marveled at how flawless my plan seemed. There was no way she would find me at the hotel. Finally, I could fully relax.

Just as anticipated, the Stein had an air-conditioned single room for me and that first afternoon I wrote, watched TV and slept. I ate dinner in the dining room almost completely alone aside from an elderly American couple who sat a few tables away. My night was highlighted by lively conversations with the kitchen staff, mostly women in their late thirties and forties. They made fun of me for staying in a hotel by myself and said it did not make sense for me to not be there with a girlfriend or wife. It felt good to laugh with them. The distraction from my situation with Deisy was more than welcome.

During my days of rest and reflection at the hotel, I did not think about Deisy or the house in the Guaduales neighborhood. It seemed futile to spend time preoccupying myself with something that was not going to change. I did not give myself permission to feel empathy toward Deisy in that moment. Grasping and accepting that reality was a process which deserved more time and required more maturity. At the time, I chose egoism.

A few days later, it was time to go to the airport and head back to Washington state. Many of the international flights leave Cali early in the morning, so I needed to take a cab from the hotel around 5:00a.m. that day. We turned onto a street in the northern part of the city, about to leave the city limits, and for a split second I thought about stopping by the Guaduales neighborhood to say goodbye to Deisy. Instead, we drove on and were at the airport a half hour later.

Just as I knelt down to take out my passport, before walking into the main entrance of the departures area, I noticed a short figure appear in my peripheral to my left. I rose slowly and Deisy stared back at me, her expression one of triumph and simultaneous despair. I immediately remembered telling her the date my flight was leaving. I had no idea how long she was waiting there, combing the crowds with her tiny eyes. I instantly felt cold. Not physically; I felt like a cold person for trying to leave the country without seeing her. We did not say anything as we walked to the escalator and into the check-in area. We also remained silent after I got my boarding pass and sat at one of the tables. I took out one of my notebooks and jotted down a message about how I hoped she would fare well until we saw each other again. I wrote that I was happy I had the chance to get to know her better. I ended the message by telling her she could still write to me whenever she wanted and that my email address would not change. As she read the paper, she shook her head slowly, wiped her eyes and we stood up to give each other a hug. I wanted to feel something, but I could not. It was not time to go to my gate yet, but I yearned for the tranquility of the other side of the security check.

* * *

My flight from Mexico City to Bogotá was delayed by a couple hours. A handful of family members and friends were going to welcome me at the Cali airport but because of the delay, I did not expect to see any of them when I arrived.

It was Christmas Day of 2009, and I just finished my last semester of undergraduate studies in southern Mexico. The university I attended had a program with a language institute in Oaxaca and it was one of the best experiences of my life. I wanted to celebrate graduation with family and friends in Cali but needed to have a quick layover in Bogotá.

We touched down in the dark in the middle of a downpour. The runway lights reflected off the pavement as I strategized my sprint to my next gate to catch my flight to Cali. Once off the plane I looked desperately for a snack to buy but everything was closed. I found my gate for the Cali flight and we were in the air in no time.

The Cali airport underwent significant changes as a multi-year remodel project was underway. Nothing was familiar from two years before except for the humidity I encountered after walking out from baggage claim. I spotted a small line of taxis to my left and began walking toward them when, all of a sudden, I felt hands and arms around my waste. I turned, ready to punch someone I thought was trying to rob me, only to see Deisy, her eyes already tearing up behind her glasses.

"*Mijo*!" she cried as she continued to hug me. I decided not to let the surprise ruin my excitement to be back in the country. I went along with her delight, hugged her back and we piled into a taxi to take us to my aunt Ana's house in the Cedro neighborhood, close to the soccer stadium in the heart of the city.

Walking up the stairs in the small house I was greeted by my two cousins, Leider and Milciades, my aunt Ana and her boyfriend, Jairo, who lived with them. I had so much I wanted to tell them about my time in Oaxaca as well as my Peace Corps assignment, which I learned was going to be in Panama. My aunt and I sat on a couch with some juice in hand along with my cousins and Jairo. Ana sipped her juice and was about to speak but hesitated. Her eyes were locked on something near the kitchen and I followed them over to Deisy, who stood with her arms folded looking at all of us. I remembered Ana explaining to me when we first met that she and Deisy did not get along but the feeling I observed in those few seconds on the couch was one of visceral abhorrence. The body language between these two women, sisters, conveyed decades of tension. The exchange only lasted a few seconds between them, with Deisy eventually moving herself into the kitchen and out of sight. What kind of fire burned between them? Did I truly want to know?

It only took two days for me to realize I could not sleep in the same space as my aunt Ana and Deisy. Their interactions escalated, becoming venomous in a way I could not have imagined. Each time I was alone with one of them, the other would speak unfavorably about her sister and say how she did not trust her, how I should not either and how I needed to be aware. Both women were merciless in their war of words and I grew tired of being caught in the crossfire. The tension was palpable. It was so toxic I could not imagine spending my entire vacation and graduation celebration enduring such heated exchanges.

I was frank in communicating my desire to leave to my aunt, and while she did not necessarily agree, she understood. A taxi took me to the gates of the Hotel Stein and just like two years before, a room was available for me. It was entertaining to reunite and joke with the kitchen staff. There was little turnover on the staff, and we picked up right where we left off.

The next morning, as I made my way into the dining room of the hotel, I smelled strong coffee and freshly sliced tropical fruits. I noticed a blond couple with a black toddler sitting by the windows. I could not recognize the language the husband and wife were speaking. I found a seat and tried not to be obvious as I continually glanced at the toddler. I assumed he was from Chiquitines since I met Chiquitines families at the hotel before.

The hotel was still very popular with adopting families as they finalized their adoptions, and I thought I had nothing to lose by introducing myself. They were not startled when I interrupted their breakfast and listened carefully as I explained my story. We were all mutually excited to meet each other. The man's name was Twan and his wife was Tamara, both from Veldhoven, a small town outside Eindhoven in The Netherlands. The toddler's name was Santiago, and they affectionately called him Santi. He was in foster care previously. We exchanged information and agreed to go out to see a bit of Cali before they headed back to Europe.

Upon returning from a short trip with friends to Medellín, I prepared plans to take Deisy out for her birthday. I wanted it to be a special day, one that we could both remember fondly. We still struggled to trust each other, but I wanted us to forget it all. She was enthusiastic about us having some time to ourselves when I went to Ana's to pick her up. I wondered when the last time was that someone took her anywhere with the sole focus being for her to enjoy herself. I did not dare ask for fear of provoking a negative emotional reaction. Instead, we summoned a taxi and headed for downtown.

I asked her, on paper, where she would like to get materials for her knitting. It was my first birthday gift to her. Her talent for knitting was unmatched. The handbags she made were particularly impressive. Two weeks prior, we discussed the possibility of turning her talent into a small business. Several family members were intrigued by the idea. It was simple enough: Deisy would teach a few other family members how to knit like she could, and together they would create elaborate handbags. My job would be to sell them in the U.S. and send the profits back to them to help them sustain themselves - family members helping family members. Eventually we would make a website and have a flourishing small business. The bags would easily sell for approximately $30-$40 USD and that represented a massive opportunity for the family, especially Deisy. We even named the idea "Hecho por Deisy" in her honor.

Once in the store, she knew exactly where to go, which materials to get and how much she needed for the handbags. We left with bags of materials, mostly yarn, and then I told her I was inviting her to lunch. I gave her the option to choose anywhere she wanted, and we ended up in a small street restaurant filled with smells of chicken soup and fresh coffee. The conversation, on napkins from my end, started off cordial, even jovial to some extent. We talked about my family back in Washington state, my goals for the coming year and when I would come back to visit Colombia. When I asked about her goals or ideas for that year, she grew silent.

Suddenly, the tears were back behind her glasses and she mumbled something under her breath. I grabbed another napkin and asked her to explain. She looked at me with her familiar lost expression, then at the ground as she said quickly, "*me tienes que ayudar a abrir una investigación para ver qué fue lo que pasó contigo. No voy a descansar hasta saber cómo y por qué te robaron*[25]*.*" I shook my head in response and, with another napkin, told her I was not going to try and do it. In my mind, an investigation would not help or change anything. Even if we were

25 You have to help me open an investigation to see what happened with you. I will not rest until I know how and why they stole you.

able to determine I was stolen, as she so fiercely insisted, what would we gain? Perhaps, she saw it as a chance to gain credibility and, simultaneously, my trust. Her timing was strange to me. Clearly, she was thinking of it all morning and afternoon.

From the time I met her in early 2005 to that moment, five years later almost to the day, she maintained the story that I was stolen from her. For the first time, I began to consider that it may be true. It infuriated me. Not because I thought I would have enjoyed a more pleasant upbringing with her than with my adoptive parents, but because it meant there may be countless other children who, like me, were stolen from their biological families. Who benefitted, especially financially, from these heartless transactions if indeed they took place?

My fourth trip to Colombia came to an end more quickly than I wanted. I was only given permission to be in the country for sixty days by the immigration official at the airport because he said I was suspicious for not having my Colombian passport yet. Nonetheless, my goals for the trip were achieved. I wanted to get to know the family better and celebrate my undergraduate graduation unapologetically. I reconnected with a lot of people from previous years, especially family members, and I got to know another part of the country. Passing through immigration at the Cali airport, yet another official scolded me for not getting my Colombian passport. Next time, he warned, they would not be so lenient, and he threatened a hefty fine. I shrugged and promised to do my best to get it taken care of next time I was in the country. He asked when that would be and again, I could only shrug. My intention was not to let another two years pass, but it turned out to be many more.

CHAPTER 9
Dual Citizen

MY EYES TEARED UP AS THE CAPTAIN ANNOUNCED WE were making our final decent into Cali. March of 2016 marked six long years since I was last in Colombia, and my emotions were as high as our plane. Before boarding my flight from Amsterdam to Cali, I initiated and then abandoned a doctorate program at the University of Bonn in Germany. The program was simply not up to the standard I expected and, after weighing my options, I decided to return to Colombia to work.

Of course, the trip was about much more than the pursuit of a paycheck. I clung to my small window in the plane snapping pictures with my phone thinking about how I was going to make Colombia my home. My quest was to belong and not simply exist as a tourist like I had during previous trips. I still wondered exactly *how* one belongs. What did it look like to participate as a citizen? In a way, I was putting Colombia through a tryout. Could Colombia earn a place in my mind as a viable option for my professional future? Did it make sense to stay long-term? I wanted to prove my Colombian-ness to myself and others. And to uncover the answers to my questions, I decided to give Colombia at least one year. After that time, I could decide whether or not to stay longer. Stepping out into the muggy evening at the airport felt amazing after having just been in chilly northern Europe and exposed to ten hours of recycled air on the plane. The breeze was light, and the familiar scent of burnt sugar cane emanated from the area surrounding the airport. I excitedly imagined what I would see, who I would meet and what I would learn in the months ahead.

For the first few weeks I only wanted to focus on reacquainting with the city. A lot had changed, especially regarding public transportation. A new bus system was implemented and the older, smaller buses with varying routes were mostly defunct. In their place were large new blue buses with air conditioning zooming around the humid streets with specific routes and large stations, many equipped with free Wi-Fi. I was shocked because in Germany Wi-Fi was such an elusive commodity. I learned quickly that Colombians are almost as obsessed with Wi-Fi as North Americans.

I spent days and nights walking to relearn the streets and made sure to reunite with family members and friends in varying parts of the city. My friend Angie, who I met back in 2004 while studying Spanish at the University Javeriana, offered to let me stay with her and her then boyfriend, Luis, while I adjusted and found my own place to live. I had my own bedroom in their apartment in the Flora neighborhood in the northern part of the city. This allowed me to move around with ease since their place was easily accessible to public transportation and a main taxi route.

I maintained a solid line of communication with my aunt Ana and a handful of cousins in Cali and Tumaco during my time in Europe via WhatsApp. My first visit was to her house and it felt as if we had just seen each other a matter of weeks before. We laughed a lot, joked with Leider and Milciades, both now well-spoken young men, and we discussed everything from family gossip to national and international politics. My other visits to see family included trips to Decepaz to see my uncle Ciro, his partner Ninfa and their daughters. The neighbors there also greeted me as family. Their living conditions had improved significantly since I last saw them and it was due to my cousin Cristian enlisting in the military. With a military uniform came consistent pay, and the house grew to three stories with a dance floor on the top level.

The first opportunity we had to use the rooftop dance floor came on my birthday the start of April. I arrived early in order to buy all the food we would need for the guests. I felt it was not fair for me to ask them to host my birthday party and not offer to pay for the food. Ninfa is a masterful cook and we walked to the store with everything she needed to orchestrate a true rooftop feast. My uncle Ciro is an enthusiastic griller, as long as he has one or two bottles of rum close by. In those neighborhoods, bottles of rum or aguardiente appear almost out of nowhere with the expectation that everyone enjoys them. Such was the case that day, as invited family members and neighbors alike flowed up the winding staircase to the breezy rooftop. Angie and Luis also came, and someone was quick to point out they were the only white people in attendance. It did not matter. The two gigantic speakers were hoisted up the stairs, the chairs were pushed to the walls and the music pulsated throughout the neighborhood. The view from the dancefloor was fantastic. It was slightly cloudy over the city, but the sun came in at an angle, throwing a blanket of gold over the brick and cement maze of the Distrito Aguablanca. We could see all the way west toward the mountains and a large portion of the city as light rain began to scatter against the tin roofs. The music only grew louder, the bottles got emptier and the dance floor more jubilant.

At one point, my cousin Briggith turned on a song I had not heard before. It was the Afro-Colombian version of the Colombian happy birthday song. The genre is called *currulao* and it has a distinctly Pacific coast sound, with all natural or handmade instruments. My cousin Dani, who was finishing up his studies to be a physical education teacher at the National Sports School, took over the dance floor as he led others in a circle of traditional *currulao* steps. He is the undisputed dancing king of the family and his last name, Alegría, matches his personality to perfection. It translates directly to 'joy'.

Joy was definitely the theme of the afternoon and evening. We did not stop dancing and joking around until well after the sun retreated behind the mountains. My uncle Ciro continued to insist that everyone take shots from another random bottle of rum and each time someone refused, he gave them a look of pity, as if they were the ones making a mistake by not drinking. His humor was the glue that kept everyone together and smiling. I got the impression he felt bored if someone was not laughing hysterically at something. As I looked around, I felt happy to know I belonged to such a united family.

All the festivities of the day came and went in such a blur that I did not have time to myself to reflect. Celebrating my birthday in Cali, with my biological family, was something I always yearned for. Of course, I would have preferred to have more family members in attendance, but fantastic memories were still created. The hardships were inevitably numerous for all of them, but that night, they hugged, danced and laughed like there would not be another day.

A few days after the unforgettable birthday party, I sat fanning myself at Ana's house in the Champagnat neighborhood. It was only about a five-minute walk from her old house where she lived six years earlier, but it was more spacious. We were sitting on her couch discussing the Colombian peace deal which developed into the main divisive issue in the country. Suddenly, the phone buzzed and signaled someone was down below. Milciades answered and the voice on the other end was unmistakable. It was Deisy asking to come up to speak to me. Word must have reached her, wherever she lived, that I returned to the city. Ana's eyes darted in my direction and somehow I knew exactly what she was about to say: "you will have to excuse me, dear, but that woman is not welcome in here. I hope you can understand." I nodded and assured her I did. The tension from six years before was still fresh in her mind and I respected her desire to not welcome more destructive vibes into her home.

Walking down the stairs, I wondered how I would react to Deisy. The tension of years past was still fresh to me as well. As I unlocked the bolt to the door and allowed my eyes adjust to the sun, there she stood with a small blue and white plastic bag in her arms. I bent down to hug her and she immediately asked if I was living with Ana. There was no form of greeting nor any smiles. I informed her on a small piece of paper I took with me from a table upstairs that I was staying with some friends in the north part of the city and instantly changed the subject. I wanted to distract her from launching into a tirade about her sister. It was important for me to know where she was living and with whom. However, I did not really know why. She reluctantly told me the address where she was staying, in a room in someone's home in the Poblado neighborhood in the far east. I pressed her for answers regarding what she had been doing for the past six years. We walked slowly to a bench down the street that was in the shade of a large tree on the sidewalk next to a corner store. She did not have a lot to report, insisting that, as per usual, she continued to survive and lamented the lack of support from her family. To avoid confrontation, I kept my thoughts to myself about how she openly rejected them at every opportunity. I only nodded and listened.

She quickly reached in her bag to pull out a few large purple grapes, an orange and some packaged crackers. "*Feliz cumpleaños, hijo.* Happy birthday, son." She said. I enthusiastically said and wrote *gracias* multiple times and gave her a hug—not because I was ecstatic about the gift, but because I knew she needed that response from me. I was doing my best to be cordial and put the layers of mistrust and animosity behind us. My intention was to start a new chapter with her. However, she must have seen right through my feeble attempt at sincerity and crossed her arms, shook her head and stared blankly at the pavement beneath us. She stopped speaking and the awkward silence of years before came rushing back. "*No entiendo por qué quieres ser un mal hijo conmigo. La única responsable de traerte al mundo soy yo*[26]." I was verbally paralyzed. There was nothing I could write to counter her penetrating words. The

26 I don't understand why you want to be a bad son with me. The only one responsible for bringing you into this world is me.

familiar feeling of wanting to get far away overcame me; I hugged her and wrote that I would go visit in the next couple of weeks. I knew it was a lie and I think she did too.

I hurried back to Ana's house after watching Deisy amble in the opposite direction. There was no need to tell her she was not welcome in her sister's home. She did not bother inquiring about it. I felt deep pity for her. In my opinion, so many things could be improved if she would accept my offer to pay for some professional psychological help. She refused years before, and I was afraid to bring the subject back up with her again. I was reminded seeking professional help for mental health was generally not something people did in Colombia, especially not those locked in the lowest socio-economic levels. And of course, trying to help someone who cannot see (or refuses to see) they need said help is often a losing battle.

Back inside the stress-free confines of Ana's living room, we resumed our conversation about politics. The topic switched to civic duties and she asked sharply if I planned to vote in the peace deal plebiscite. I reveled in the idea of voting for the first time in Colombia. It was another way I wanted to establish a sense of belonging in the country. However, there were bureaucratic hurdles standing in the way. My names alone were cause enough for confusion to anyone who asked to see my Colombian ID. It was time to change my paperwork.

Seattle does not have a Colombian consulate. The closest one is in San Francisco so in order for Colombians living in the Pacific Northwest to complete consular transactions, it is necessary to travel to the Bay area or up to Vancouver B.C. I flew to the Bay Area in 2013 to acquire my Colombian ID. At the consulate, we had to call the notary where my Colombian birth certificates were located, in Cali, to have them fax us original copies of the documents. In them, my complete name was Alfonso Taylor Nygard. I was confused because my original Colombian passport as a baby read Alfonso Mosquera. Why did the names not match between my birth certificate and my passport, the official document to leave Colombia? I learned there were two sets of birth certificates. One had my original name and the other had my original first name with my adoptive surnames. In Colombia and most of Latin America, the father's last name comes first, followed by the mother's maiden name. The consulate said they could only order a cédula for me with the names Alfonso Taylor Nygard, even though I tried to insist that my name match my U.S. documents. They countered that I needed to do an official name change but that such a procedure could only be completed within Colombia's borders.

I never imagined I would be in a situation that required the legal changing of my name. Yet, there I stood in line at the Sixth Notary in downtown Cali. The process itself seemed simple enough. I needed to provide my cédula from the San Francisco consulate, my copies of the birth certificates and the copies of my adoption documents because I knew they would have questions. And sure enough, the woman who helped me make copies of my paperwork and sign an authorization form asked frankly, "*y por qué ya no quieres ser norteamericano*[27]*?*" I corrected her, saying I simply sought to have my Colombian passport and proof of my dual citizenship. I had no aspirations of abandoning either of my nationalities.

Receiving our cédula and passports is a sort of rite of passage for Colombian adoptees. When I walked out of the office

27 And why don't you want to be North American anymore?

after picking up my passport, I stood in the humidity holding it and flipping through the blank pages. I was elated. For many of us, our passport confirms our status as citizens of the country, even if legally we had the citizenship all along. There is boundless value in holding a tangible manifestation of citizenship. For countless adoptees, it is the culmination of years, even decades, of questions relating to identity and belonging. It is to emphatically declare, "I am seen now. Those who question me have no choice but to recognize me. Therefore, I belong."

As I began to feel more comfortable with my knowledge of the streets and neighborhoods, I reached out to find volunteer opportunities. Volunteering developed into an important part of my adult life and I wanted to contribute to an organization I really believed in. Luckily, my friend Maritza Jiménez took me to the Cali branch of SOS Children's Villages, an international non-profit organization that provides services and housing for impoverished youth growing up without parental support or protection. Maritza was a teacher at Chiquitines when I volunteered there with Daniela back in 2004 and we remained friends via social media.

We arrived at the gates to *Aldeas*, as it was locally called, short for *Aldeas Infantiles*, in the Prados del Sur neighborhood. Brick and concrete homes covered the hills around the Aldeas grounds. Laundered clothes, linens and Colombian flags hung from windows and the occasional palm tree sprouted up amongst the dusty maze of houses. Motorcycles buzzed up and down the street and neighbors called to each other in the street, reminding me of Decepaz. Once inside the gate, Maritza was proud to introduce me to a small handful of teenagers who were in Chiquitines as babies and toddlers, one of whom I recognized from one of my visits to the orphanage. To her knowledge, they were the only kids in Aldeas from Chiquitines. The rest were protected by the national child welfare system. At Aldeas, four or five kids lived in a small brick home together and a middle-aged woman was their caregiver, along with the rest of the staff and administrators. The director popped in to introduce himself and I felt an immediate connection. He was hilarious and very welcoming. His name was Hernán and although he lived in Cali for a number of years, he still clung to his thick Medellín accent.

Maritza initiated a conversation about how I could get involved volunteering with Aldeas with Hernán and a few other staff members. Eventually, we decided I could teach the staff English and also support some of the kids there who were studying English. It was an exciting opportunity, even though I had not taught English for a few years. Shortly after our meeting, Hernán gave me a tour of the organization and introduced me to numerous kids and staff members. He provided them with a brief summary of my story and was sure to include the fact that I was from Chiquitines. It seemed to gain me immediate credibility with the staff and kids alike. Within fifteen minutes I was invited to two birthday celebrations and a soccer game with the kids.

My volunteer duties were established just a few weeks before I started my first job. Before leaving Germany, I applied to work with the Colombian Ministry of Education's Colombia Bilingüe program. It was the former Education Minister's initiative aimed at providing public schools throughout the country with native English-speaking assistants in English classes. Generally, having access to native speakers of languages other than Spanish were reserved for private school students throughout the country. I was attracted to the program because it seemed like the government was finally beginning to take education more seriously than it had in the past. In my research, I learned it was the first time in Colombian history the education budget was larger than the military budget. However miniscule my contribution, I wanted to be a part of that effort.

At the orientation, I met the other English Fellows and we were assigned the schools we would work in. Fellows came from a variety of countries and were sent all over Colombia to schools in some of the most impoverished neighborhoods in the cities. Mine was the Celmira Bueno de Orejuela school, located in the Chiminangos neighborhood in the northeastern part of the city. My role was to assist an English teacher with her classes and find ways to create an English-speaking club with another Fellow.

Prior to my arrival, the students were told a Fellow was coming from the U.S. The morning I walked into the school for the first time, I was met with stares from everyone in the small courtyard. They knew who I was, but their faces were frozen with confusion. "*Ese man no parece gringo, parece caleño*[28]*!*" I heard one of the older students say as I walked to the administration office to introduce myself to staff members. Indeed, I did not fit the stereotypical appearance of someone from the U.S., but I said, "good morning" and "hello" in English to all the kids I shook hands with. I figured we would have time to discuss my background when the opportunity presented itself.

I will never forget the moment I met the class I would work with. The teacher and I met at the orientation for the program and as I walked into the classroom, the open-air brick walled room fell silent. The teacher stood up from her desk at the front

---

28 That guy doesn't look like a gringo, he looks like he's from Cali!

of the room to introduce me. One of the first things she said was how disappointed she was that I did not have blond hair and blue eyes, but that she was certain I would do a good job. She meant it as a joke, but I found it unprofessional and in poor taste. I cut her off from something else she started to say by saying thank you in English while motioning with my hand she could let me speak. I launched into roughly a two-minute introduction in Spanish, intentionally using local slang as I walked slowly around the humid classroom.

The kids, especially those in the back on their phones, perked up immediately. They were not expecting their new English Fellow to speak to them in Colombian Spanish. I explained the basics of my story so they could understand where I was coming from. Fellows were supposed to communicate exclusively in English with our students, but I wanted to be sure they understood who I was in order to establish a level of trust before we started with our academic tasks. I made it a point to learn each of their names, approximately thirty-seven in total, that afternoon. After school was out, I spent an hour meeting with different groups of students in front of the small fountain in the courtyard. A general sense of trust was established that first day with teachers and students alike. It set the foundation for an excellent experience.

Ironically, my quest for a deeper sense of belonging in Colombia was not going to be achieved without dedicating significant energy to helping others belong as well. This became most obvious as I began to understand my students and their perceptions of the world. A select group of them had advanced English skills but complained almost daily about the Chiminangos neighborhood and their tedious routines.

One day, I asked them why they opted not to do something to alter the monotony. They stared back at me blankly, almost as if I offended them. "*Y qué piensas que podemos hacer entonces*[29]*?*" one of them asked in a demanding tone. Since they all wanted to get out of the neighborhood more often, I suggested they go on small field trips around the city. Cali is filled with a collection of parks and there are always opportunities to attend cultural activities. Again, I was met with blank stares. Almost at the same time, as if it were a rehearsed response, they started making excuses about how there was nothing to see or do. Cali was too dangerous. Cali did not have a nice metro system like Medellín. Cali was too poor. Cali did not have a beach and so on. I stopped them and asked why they were so eager to provide me with excuses. I described how many interesting and fun things I had seen in the city and how there were multiple places to socialize and learn new things at the same time. I had their attention. My impulse got the best of me and I blurted, without considering logistics, that I would take them somewhere as long as we practiced their English skills. "*De una*![30]" they exclaimed in unison. The more I thought about it, the more it made sense to take them to different parts of the city away from their neighborhood. We would explore Cali, but in order to get them around more English speakers and foreigners in general, I would need to take them to the San Antonio neighborhood.

San Antonio is, in a word, eclectic. It is the most popular neighborhood for tourists who come to the city to learn the Cali style of salsa dancing. It boasts an extensive park at the top of a hill with arguably the best view in the city. There are multiple

---

29 And what do you think we can do then?

30 Colombian slang for "alright!"

cafes, restaurants, bakeries and bars featuring international flavors as well as typical Colombian snacks. It is almost dizzying looking at all the graffiti art on the walls throughout the neighborhood. It is also home to countless hostels, each with a unique painted theme, many with a built-in dancefloor. To top it all off, San Antonio is the local colonial neighborhood and city government officials have made the effort to preserve the colorful one and two-story buildings with brick tile rooftops. My students never went there because, in their opinion, they did not want to hang out with "hippies and gringos." I challenged them to get out of their comfort zones. They could expand their world vision by simply walking around and hearing people from other parts of the world. They accepted the challenge and we went there on multiple occasions to eat French crepes and practice English. I was happy to hear them reflect that our small trips and conversations helped them feel more at home in their own city. They reported that exploring the city and striking up conversations with foreigners made them feel prouder of the region but, perhaps more importantly, allowed them to develop a deeper "*sentido de pertinencia con la ciudad*, sense of belonging", as one of them pointed out.

November arrived and I cancelled one of our trips because I needed to visit Deisy in the Poblado neighborhood. With a renewed sense of urgency to find my biological father, my mission was to pull more information out of her in order to conduct a more productive search. While I sat next to her on a bed in the home she was living in, I changed the subject of conversation to my biological father. I wanted to see if she would maintain the same details of their time together including his name. Because of the strained relationship, the countless lies from years before, I assumed there would be holes in her story. I flipped to a new page in the small notebook and wrote that I wanted to hear about her time with my biological father again, including all the details she could remember. She looked astonished and scolded me for not remembering. "*Ya te expliqué todo, nada ha cambiado*[31]", she snapped in her unique, squeaky tone as she folded her arms, turning her face away from me. I waited a few seconds without writing anything and she began to tell her stories. She was right. Nothing about what she told me years before changed. She added a new detail about them being together for five or six months. Everything else was the same as before: his name, José Quiñones Ríos, his profession as a teacher and his affinity for alcohol. I paid close attention and took extensive mental notes because, although I would not tell her, I plotted to begin a serious search for him. I decided it would be best to update her as I made progress, little by little. This made the most sense to me because, knowing her, inevitably she would demand to help. The last thing I wanted was to find her following me around the city again, which could have happened if I brought her directly into the search effort. Then she changed the subject, launching into a rant about me needing to call and write to her more. I listened to her lecture me about how I needed to be more grateful and respect her more. Maybe she was right, but my patience for her thirst for drama ran out. I gave her a hug, told her I would see her soon and was out the door in a matter of minutes.

Searching for my biological father presented one large obstacle: he did not know I existed. I was not sure how to begin the process, I just knew it had to happen. I imagined that José,

---

31 I already explained everything to you. Nothing has changed.

if that was indeed his name, lived his life every day with no idea he has a son, let alone in another country. To launch my search, I wanted to get the word out as much as I could. It would take a much greater effort than simply posting on social media and holding out hope.

My first thought was to contact local and regional journalists to solicit their help. I already had a contact at the Caracol Television network because of my work translating and transcribing files for one of their national programs. Unfortunately, they said, they could not help with my search. I reached out via email to a host of regional and other national news outlets. Weeks passed with no response, until one afternoon, when I received a call from an unknown number. The woman on the other end called from a local radio station in Cali and said they would be happy to give me a short live interview. My email address was forwarded to her from someone from one of the local newspapers I reached out to. I accepted her offer and participated in an interview that was about five minutes long. When I arrived at the radio station office, I realized it was a highly religious organization and at the conclusion of the interview, the two young women interviewing me spent ten minutes trying to recruit me to their church.

The next opportunity to get the word out about José came in the form of another radio interview with Aldemar Dominguez, a contact of my friend Monica Bolaños. Like my friend Maritza, Monica worked as a teacher at Chiquitines years before. Monica helped to arrange for a phone interview during a live radio show called Viva Las Noticias, and I was pleased to have a lengthy conversation. Both radio interviews would get wide coverage across the city, but I felt it was necessary to have regional and potentially national exposure. Luckily, one of my coworkers at the Celmira Bueno de Orejuela school had a girlfriend who was a journalist for the regional newspaper, El País. Her name was Paola and after messaging with her for a bit, we decided to do a phone interview and she would write an article for the online version of the paper. Her supervisors approved it and we were off and running.

Paola's article made its way across multiple social media platforms for a little over a week. It was a complete description of my story and of my desire to find José. My friends, colleagues, family members and even a handful of students, helped to spread it as far as possible. I was optimistic that someone would come forward with a piece of information regarding the man I had launched a national campaign to locate. However, neither that email nor that phone call never came, and I felt defeated. It would take a doctor appointment to reignite any optimism.

When I first arrived in Colombia from Germany, I was severely dehydrated and endured what was diagnosed as a dissolving kidney stone. My appointment for a follow-up after about a year arose and I was once again in the northern part of the city waiting to see the specialist, Dr. Echeverri.

He welcomed me in his office with a firm handshake, and we spent about five minutes talking about potentially lingering symptoms. He changed the subject, apologizing for never getting in touch about the possibility of tutoring his son to improve his English. The conversation switched again to soccer and then, out of nowhere, he asked if I could explain my last names. He knew I was adopted from my previous appointments but wanted more details. *"Definitivamente tu primer apellido es gringo y el segundo es muy colombiano. Mosquera es de tu padre biológico*[32]*?"* he asked calmly. I shook my head and explained to him it was from my biological mother. He nodded slightly and continued: *"y qué de tu padre biológico*[33]*?"* I shrugged and told him I was searching but did not have any information or even any leads about him. The only information I had was his name.

Dr. Echeverri perked up and smiled. He turned to his computer and demanded to know the name, his fingers already resting on the keyboard. He noticed my confused expression and, in a tranquil tone, said we could try to find my biological father in his medical database. It seemed like a brilliant idea. I told him the names I had, and he typed the first last name ending with a Z (Quiñonez). No results emerged on the screen. I corrected him and said it most likely ended with an 'S'. He typed José Quiñones Rios and sure enough, one result jumped onto the bright blue screen in small white text. He clicked on the name and the individual's contact information, birthdate, cédula number, insurance company and place of employment were all present.

"Anota la información y llama[34]*!"* barked Dr. Echeverri, beaming with the satisfaction of having potentially helped. The birthdate certainly made sense since Deisy told me she was slightly older than my biological father. The place of origin also made sense. It stated this José was from Sevilla, a smaller city in the northern part of the Valle del Cauca department. This was important because again, according to what Deisy told me, my biological father was from "somewhere close to Pereira and

---

32 Your first last name is definitely American and the second is very Colombian. Mosquera is from your biological father?

33 And what about your biological father?

34 Take down the information and call!

would always talk about it." Sevilla is not far from the city of Pereira. Dr. Echeverri laughed as he studied my dumbfounded expression. He gave me a high-five and instructed me to let him know how the search went. Could it really have been that simple? From just one click on a screen I suddenly had access to the only candidate in the country I thought that could be my biological father.

Excitement overcame me and as I walked outside from the clinic and dialed the house number I jotted down. After several rings, there was no answer. I checked the number and dialed again with both hands mildly trembling. An elderly woman picked up this time and I asked immediately for José. She insisted I had the wrong number and abruptly hung up. Again, I checked the number and dialed. The same woman answered. Same response. Click. I was far from deterred. If anything, I felt a fire reignite in me. However, the street was no place to formulate a different approach. I hailed a taxi back to my apartment and pondered how I could find a way to communicate with José.

A few days of contemplation passed, and I decided to try to contact José's place of employment in Bogotá. It was a paper and packaging company. However, their website was last updated ten years earlier. I tried sending a message to the only email address I could find associated with the company and it came back saying it was an invalid address. I tried calling the two different phone numbers available on the website as well. Both numbers were disconnected. My hope began to deteriorate once again. It appeared there was no way to locate or contact José. The visit to Dr. Echeverri's office did not yield any cell phone numbers or personal email addresses. There was no home mailing address either. My initial elation was reduced to piercing frustration. There was nothing more that could be done aside from waiting for the article and radio interviews to produce something. Days turned to weeks and the possibility of someone reaching out to me with any useful information slipped further and further away.

By that time, I was well into my second teaching venture at the Colegio Bennett, one of the prestigious private schools in the southern part of Cali. It was a full-time teaching position and not a program sponsored by the national government like the one at the Celmira Bueno de Orejuela school. I went from being essentially an exasperated English teaching assistant to having my own air-conditioned classroom where I taught introductory philosophy to high schoolers and world history to eighth graders. I had never taught either subject before, nor did I have extensive coursework in my undergraduate or graduate programs on the subjects. It was a fantastic opportunity to expand my abilities and my students, similarly to my public-school students in the north, were enthusiastic to have a young and energetic instructor. I promptly made a few friends on the faculty and staff, one who particularly stood out.

María del Pilar Gutiérrez was a psychologist by profession and worked as the school's quality coordinator. When we sat for lunch in the school's cafeteria for the first time, she explained how she and her husband adopted their son, Samuel, from Chiquitines. "*Así que ustedes dos son como hermanos*[35]." She said smiling. We met a few more times for lunch as the semester winded to a close and each time we found ourselves talking about our philosophies surrounding adoption. María del Pilar had a calming voice and was very inquisitive. Our conversations

35 So, you two are like brothers.

reached above and beyond that of two colleagues with a couple things in common. In a way, we became each other's mentors. She guided me on the intricacies of working and surviving in one of Cali's distinguished schools and I helped her anticipate possible obstacles Samuel might face in the future. It was a great exchange and the best would come after I began to conclude my time in the country.

I spent those final weeks making various trips around the city to say *adios* and *gracias* to everyone who was a part of my life during my year and four months stay in Cali. I met with my students from the Celmira Bueno de Orejuela school, the Aldeas staff and kids, multiple friends from years past as well as family members. I really felt as if I achieved my goal of feeling a sense of belonging in the city. I knew all the bus routes, rented an apartment, held a bank account, worked, volunteered and developed a sense of pride in the many positive ways the city was growing. I saw hope in my students. I saw resilience in the Aldeas kids. Above all, I felt more comfortable than ever with my extended biological family. The bond we created and the trust that emerged from it, at least for me, was the crowning achievement of all the weeks and months spent there.

Everything came full circle for me during my final week before heading back up to the Seattle area. María del Pilar summoned me via text message for another lunch at the school cafeteria.

"*Te gustaría venir a hablar con padres adoptivos sobre tus experiencias y ofrecerles tu perspectiva? Tienes muchas cosas por ofrecer*[36]." She went on to explain how she was part

36 Would you like to come speak with adoptive parents about your experiences and offer your perspective? You have a lot of things to offer.

of an association of adoptive parents, called Alamor, and they would like host a Q&A session for me if I was willing. It seemed like the perfect way to culminate my time in Colombia. If I could give back to Colombian adoptive parents by sharing my experiences to help them understand just a little bit of what adoptees go through, it was an opportunity I had to seize.

The pavement was scorching as I stepped out of the taxi at the location Alamor had reserved for our small event. María del Pilar and Samuel were there to greet me as eventgoers arrived in their cars and taxis. We made small talk as we walked up brick stairs to a rooftop overlooking the southern and western parts of the city. I was almost blinded by the reflection of the sun off of nearby windows. The sweat was already reaching through my white button-up shirt, yet it was not due to the humidity. I was nervous! I wanted to make a great and lasting impression on the couples in attendance. Once inside, the air conditioning provided fantastic relief. There were four long white plastic tables arranged in a rectangle and covered with white and blue tablecloths. A single microphone stood at the head table along with multiple glass jars of water. White plastic chairs were arranged around the tables and signs advertising Alamor hung at the front of the room.

Almost thirty people sat at the tables sipping their waters and fanning themselves even as the air conditioning raged. María del Pilar gave an eloquent introduction and then turned the microphone over to me to discuss my experiences growing up in the U.S. However, I did not want to simply talk about myself, I wanted to hear questions from the group. It seemed like a better use of our time to have a conversation instead of a presentation. They welcomed my approach and the first question

I received was about how comfortable I felt in Colombia. It was such a timely question since I was mulling it over in my head for the past couple of weeks prior.

Articulating what I felt about my time in the city was an easy task. I explained that I established a better relationship with my biological family, and I felt at home there. Obviously, I went on, the main component in that process was taking steps to master the language. They nodded and then a man sitting toward the front, to my left, motioned for the microphone that was being passed between the guests. He wore a light pink button-up shirt, glasses and I could not tell if the moisture on his forehead was sweat or the gel leaking down his face from his pointed short black hair. In any case, he described how much he loved his child and how he and his family could not be happier with their situation. He went on like this for a few moments and finally asked why he should eventually tell his child that they were adopted. He argued it was too much of a headache for everyone involved and that too many problems could come from their knowing the truth about their origin. "*Usted como adoptado qué nos puede decir al respecto*[37]*?*" he pleaded, clearly passionate about the decision he made about never revealing the truth to his child.

I found two things uncomfortable about what this man requested. First, he was essentially demanding me to speak on behalf of all adoptees everywhere. Doing so is an impossible feat. Our philosophies surrounding adoption are not universal and our experiences are nuanced. There certainly can be certain themes that may apply to our collective lived experiences, but they are far from identical. The second, and perhaps more important contributor to my discomfort, was his contentment at

---

37 As an adopted person, what can you tell us about that?

concealing the truth from his child for the duration of their lifetime. He seemed so cavalier about it; his smirk etched comfortably on his tanned face. It flew in the face of transparency and, in my opinion, was simply not fair to the child. Not fair to us.

The truth is what belonging is all about. That man's child, and all adoptees, including myself, deserve to have that truth in order to understand our place in this world – to cultivate our sense of individualism and belonging. In a way, to belong to ourselves. The truth allows us to feel comfortable in our own skin. It is our irrefutable right and it is each adoptive parents' duty to provide all the information possible surrounding our past and places of origin. Anything less is a feckless attempt at cowardice. And for what? To ease the experiences of the adoptive parent while their child lives a life weighed down by a lie—forever trapped by the confines of their parents' egocentric apathy? I don't think so.

I held the microphone in my right hand, resting atop the table, as I felt the attention of the room focus on me. It was the most nervous I had been in a while and it showed as my hand quivered and I brought the microphone to my lips.

"*Señor*", I began after taking a deep breath, "*con todo respeto, no estoy de acuerdo con lo que dijo. Todos tenemos derecho a saber nuestra verdad*[38]."

---

38 Sir, with all due respect, I do not agree with what you said. We all have a right to know our truth.

EPILOGUE

I SAT UP ABRUPTLY IN BED AS MY EYES ADJUSTED TO the morning light jumping through my apartment blinds, my pulse thumping at an accelerated rate. An email in my phone's inbox read, "Your reports are ready." It was from 23andMe. The three-week long wait for my DNA results was finally over.

My sole intention for participating in the popular DNA test was to understand more about my ancestry. Admittedly, I had not read about the extensive information provided when one receives their results from the lab, so after scrolling through the various percentages which make up my ethnic background, I was shocked to see an option to select a box which read "one close relative." After tapping the box, more out of curiosity than any misplaced expectation, I was taken to a new screen with a small picture of a man named Luis Fernando Ramirez Echeverri with the words 'second cousin' next to his name. Luis Fernando was almost as white as the background on the screen. How could he possibly be a second cousin if my entire biological family was black? Then it hit me: Luis Fernando was my best new lead regarding the search for my biological father because Deisy always insisted he was a white man.

Aside from the 'second cousin' label, there was no further detail as to how exactly Luis Fernando and I were related, but I did not need additional information. The science confirmed we shared a biological connection, and I immediately made it my mission to find out exactly how. The search for my biological father was unexpectedly revived.

Ironically, the 23andMe results came on Sunday February third of 2018, less than two months since I had decided to give up on the search altogether. In early January of that same year, I felt myself sink as I told curious friends and family in both of my countries the hunt for Mr. Quiñones was over. I was prepared to abandon the search entirely after a different DNA test failed to provide favorable results in Bogotá.

Back in July of 2017, when I left Colombia after my year and four months stay, I was undecided if I would continue my search for my biological father. The effort the media outlets made was significant but yielded no results. Sometime before Christmas of that year, I randomly decided to search for the man with the names from the doctor visit in Cali on social media and found him. He did not respond to my friend request or message with a brief note about the desire to speak with him about something 'important'. It was important not to drop the bomb of 'you could be my biological father' on him in that message. There was no response for weeks. I guessed someone close to him might respond, so I looked at a few of his pictures. There was a woman, named Layda*[39], in all of them who I assumed was his wife. I messaged her and she responded within ten minutes. I made clear that I was not looking for money. I struggled to find the words to ask Layda, essentially, if José had ever slept with a black woman in Cali in the 80s. There was the very real possibility of an extramarital affair, especially after Layda told me they were married for thirty-eight years. My thirty-fifth birthday was just around the corner. The math was not in her favor.

39 * Name changed

After some time messaging back and forth, we all spoke via social media and initially, José was decidedly resistant to taking a DNA test. I offered to pay for one I found online for $80 USD and told them we could have the results within eight days. He still refused. Layda pressed him to collaborate and finally he cracked, telling me in a separate phone call that if I wanted to do a DNA test, I would need to go to Bogotá and we would do it there. He said he feared I would manipulate the results if he sent a DNA sample to a lab in the United States. I thought it was absurd, especially because I knew I would not be back in Colombia until the following December, another year from that moment.

Over the course of that year I endured Layda's late-night texts, venting about how she felt José cheated on her multiple times and how she would be surprised if I was the only child he had outside of their marriage. For a year he kept her, their three sons and me in suspense.

When I finally boarded the plane from Seattle to Houston and then on to Bogotá in December of 2018, I felt more annoyed than anxious or curious. We could have had the results a year before but of course, I could not force Juan to take any tests. It was not easy, but I had to respect his position. My plane touched down around 6:30a.m. in Bogotá and we agreed after I checked in at my hotel, I would take a taxi directly to their house. A few friends in the U.S. as well as in Colombia expressed concern about my choice to visit a stranger's home in the sprawling capital. Some criticized me for being naïve. I dismissed their words of caution and blindly focused on the DNA test.

José and Layda were very welcoming. Layda opened her arms wide and squeezed tightly as we exchanged light pleasantries when I walked through their door. I felt welcomed and at ease in their living room sipping on some fruit juice. Speaking with José, however, was another story. He fidgeted constantly with his fingers and avoided eye contact with me. He was clearly uncomfortable. I am sure if I were in his position, I would act the same. All the pressure was squarely on his shoulders and he knew it.

The time came to leave, and we piled into their small red car and sped towards the downtown area to take the DNA test at one of the local clinics. When we pulled up, Layda was stopped at the door by the security guard. His instructions were for anyone not being tested to remain outside. She hissed at him, his chiseled face showed no change in expression and he motioned for her to take a seat on a nearby bench. José and I stepped through the single glass door and sat down almost at the same time in two black leather chairs. We noticed each other rubbing our own upper arms to stay warm because the lobby was frigid. The young receptionist called our names and asked who would pay. I rose my hand and she motioned for me to come to her desk while momentarily waving a white pen in the air. The final price was the equivalent of nearly $200 USD, much more than the original price of the test I tried to convince José to take a year earlier. I let out a sigh of frustration before emptying my wallet. I exchanged money at the airport earlier that morning but did not anticipate the price would be so high. "*Estás nervioso*?" José asked as he frantically wiped his palms on his slacks. I told him no, that I had nothing to be nervous about since my life was not going to change dramatically with a positive or negative result. He was clearly nervous but maintained a stoic demeanor, insisting there was no reason for him to be nervous about something he knew to be a waste of time.

We were summoned into a smaller room immediately to our right with the windows covered in solid white plastic tarp. A petite pale woman with a white mask, long black hair and thick brown glasses sat behind a small wooden table and commanded us to sit. There were no pleasantries or small talk. We were instructed to look at a camera because they needed to take images of our eyes and facial structure. Then we were fingerprinted. Finally, our thumbs were pricked individually, and a sample of our blood was dripped onto thin white strips. We were done. Since I would already be back in Seattle by the time the results would be ready, they said José needed to return after his vacation to the Caribbean coast to pick them up. He agreed. Layda assured me they would send me pictures of the documents once they had them in their hands. I trusted her.

However, after almost three weeks of waiting, Layda sent me a message with a picture. There were no words with her message, just a bright picture taken of the document with the DNA results which read, "NO HAY COMPATIBILIDAD ENTRE LOS DOS PACIENTES[40]." The man I spent so much time and effort to find and convince to complete a DNA test was, in fact, not my biological father. I felt deflated yet also relieved because José and I could not be more opposite. That test was the culmination of all my efforts, and it felt as though there was no more wind in my sail.

Throughout the DNA testing period with José and Layda, I kept my word to my former doctor in Cali, Dr. Echeverri, and updated him on the developments. It felt like the right thing

---

40 There is no compatibility between the two patients.

to do since he was so generous to help me in his office that day regarding the search for my biological father. Our communication was sporadic because of our busy lives but when we finally connected in mid-February of 2019, I flooded his social media direct message inbox with details about contacting a second cousin through 23andMe in the city of Armenia. He wasted no time with any sort of congratulations and immediately asked for the names of the people I found, insisting he had friends and family in Armenia who might be able to help. It took only a few seconds after me typing Luis Fermando's full name for Dr. Echeverri to respond flatly, "yes, I know him. He's a cousin of mine too."

It was mind-boggling to me how the doctor I met randomly in a medical clinic in northern Cali a year and half earlier ended up being related to the person I found on a DNA website. Though somewhat distantly, this confirmed that he and I were also biologically connected. I was beside myself. Dr. Echeverri remained relaxed and calmly suggested we meet for a drink next time I was in Colombia.

Luis Fernando and the handful of his family members who have reached out to me via social media are the only hope I have of locating my biological father. They have been cordial and are willing to do everything possible to help me. Deisy has offered no assistance since the last time we saw each other in November of 2016. She lost credibility in my eyes to the point where I now doubt everything she told me regarding my biological father. I no longer believe they spent months together during the time of my conception or that he was a teacher. There is also no evidence suggesting his name is even José, Quiñones or Ríos.

The only option I have now is to wait. It will take months and perhaps even years for word of the story you hold in your hands to reach my biological father – if he is indeed still alive. If he is, I look forward to the day we can sit down over a coffee and discuss what it means to belong in each other's lives.

ACKNOWLEDGEMENTS

IT IS A SINGULAR HONOR TO OFFER MY MOST SINCERE thanks to the individuals who have supported me throughout this process. I simply could not have begun to fathom writing a book without their consistent demonstrations of encouragement.

When I think of who to publicly thank, my first thoughts drift to my immediate family. Specifically, I am referring to my parents, Tim and Cindy Taylor, my sister Diana and my grandparents, Harry and Marge Nygard. Each of them, in their own unique ways, contributed to me developing my understanding of the world. My parents and grandparents are the architects of any success, personal or professional, that I have been able to enjoy. I love them with everything I am and everything I will be.

Someone said friends are the family one chooses. Thankfully, my chosen family is extensive but there are a handful of them who were instrumental in the completion of this project.

Daniela Metal and I introduce each other to third parties as siblings. I refer to Gloria, her resilient mother, as my Colombian mom. To both of them I extend a heartfelt *gracias* for bringing me into their family and for guiding me with my first steps and words in our other country.

Aaron Dufault is a close friend of twenty-two years. His magnificent wife, Molly, read, revised, critiqued and edited I Met Myself in October: A Memoir of Belonging. Her insight was fundamental in ensuring the memoir developed into a cohesive and engaging text. And their little daughter Cora helped too!

Isaac Martinez has been one of my closest friends for the past twenty years. A savvy graphic designer, Isaac was instrumental in the beginning stages of developing the cover.

Others involved in the reading and editing process spanned across different states and countries, reaching as far as The Netherlands, South Africa and England. In London, Nat Illumine leaned on her experience as an editor for the online multimedia journal Afropean, which explores social and cultural intersections of the African diaspora in Europe. She also edited I Met Myself in October: A Memoir of Belonging and, like those mentioned before, offered valuable advice for moving the project forward. In the Netherlands, my Dutch/Haitian 'sister', Isabelle De Roux, helped to read and edit a couple chapters. *Dank je wel!*

I thank Patricia Delgadillo, Carrie Ann Gillispie, Pilar Mendoza, Hans Villamil and Melissa Weizman for their assistance in revising and editing select chapters as well as providing imperative insight regarding marketing for the memoir project.

In Colombia, I am grateful to Isabella Sinisterra for help with chapter eight but also for caring for me during my time in the Chiquitines Adoption Center all those years ago before I was placed for adoption. I thank Agatha León for leading that institution for as long as she did and for her assistance with chapter one. In addition, I appreciate Maria del Pilar Gutiérrez's help with chapter nine along with her mentorship and friendship.

A mi familia biológica en Cali y Tumaco: mil gracias por todo su cariño y su apoyo durante estos últimos dieciséis años. Juntos, hemos logrado muchas cosas lindas y nos esperan momentos aún más mágicos. Lo he dicho en varias ocasiones: me siento orgulloso de ser parte de ustedes. Los quiero mucho.

To the two women in charge of finalizing my adoption process, Mary Ann Curran and Karen Olson, I thank them for their years of dedicated service at the organization formerly known as World Association of Children and Parents.

Finally, I want to acknowledge my ever-expanding network of adoptees. They have been there for me in more ways than I can count. With all of them, I stand in firm solidarity.

I feel fortunate to have each of them in my life as we navigate our different paths of belonging.

ABOUT THE AUTHOR

JACOB TAYLOR-MOSQUERA IS AN ENTHUSIASTIC people connector in the extensive international adoption community. He regularly networks, promotes and participates in adoption-related events in the Pacific Northwest in the United States. Jacob also simultaneously provides informal cultural and linguistic consulting to other Latin American adoptees across the U.S., Europe and Australia. He completed his undergraduate studies at Pacific Lutheran University in Tacoma, Washington and his master's degree at the Universiteit Leiden in Leiden, Netherlands.

In addition, Jacob is the Head of Spanish Language Communications at DecodingOrigins.com, a website for the anthology titled Decoding our Origins: The Lived Experiences of Colombian Adoptees. The book was written by seventeen Colombian adoptees living across multiple countries. The contributing authors aim to help Colombian adoptees search for and reunite with their biological families by purchasing DNA test kits with the proceeds from the anthology.

You can follow Jacob and the next steps for his debut book, I Met Myself in October: A Memoir of Belonging, on the following pages:

Official memoir website with blog:
www.imetmyselfmemoir.com
Facebook: I Met Myself in October: A Memoir of Belonging
Instagram: @profejacobtm
Twitter: @JTaylorMosquera